Story Keepers

Conversations with Aboriginal Writers

2004

Funding provided by National Literacy Secretariat and Ontario Arts Council.

Library and Archives Canada Cataloguing in Publication

David, Jennifer
     Story keepers : conversations with aboriginal writers/ by Jennifer David.

Includes bibliographical references.
ISBN 978-1-896832-51-7

     1. Indian authors—Canada—Interviews. 2. Authors, Canadian— 20th century—Interviews. 3. Canadian literature—Indian authors— History and criticism. I. Title.

PS8089.5.I6D38 2005   C810.9'897
C2005-900143-7

Published by:

Ningwakwe Learning Press
www.ningwakwe.on.ca
Owen Sound ON
Canada

2004

Table of Contents

Sources

Acknowledgements for previously published material as reference sources in this book appear here:

Richard Van Camp's books:
Angel Wing Splash Pattern, **Kegedonce Press.**
The Lesser Blessed, **Douglas and McIntyre**
A Man Called Raven, **Children's Book Press.**

Drew Hayden Taylor's books :
Baby Blues and Only Drunks and Children Tell the Truth, **Talonbooks**
Funny You Don't Look Like One, **Theytus Books**, Penticton.
Someday, **Fifth House Ltd.**, Calgary.

Ruby Slipperjack's books:
Honour the Sun, **Pemmican Publications**
Silent Words, **Fifth House Ltd.**, Calgary.
Weesquachak and the Lost Ones, **Theytus Books**, Penticton.
Little Voice, **Coteau Books**, Regina.

Gregory Scofield's books:
Thunder Through My Veins, **HarperFlamingoCanada.**
Native Canadiana, I Knew Two Metis Women, Love Medicine and One Song, **Polestar.**

Lee Maracle's books:
Bobbi Lee, Indian Rebel, **Women's Press**, Toronto.
I Am Woman, Sojourners and Sundogs, Ravensong, **Press Gang**, Vancouver.
Daughters are Forever, **Polestar**, Vancouver.
Bent Box, **Theytus Books**, Penticton.

Louise Halfe's books:
Coteau Books, Regina.

Basil Johnston's books:
Indian School Days, Crazy Dave, **Key Porter Books**.
Moose Meat and Wild Rice, **McClelland and Stewart.**

Jeannette Armstrong's books:
Theytus Books, Penticton.

Armand Ruffo's books:
Opening in the Sky, **Theytus Books**, Penticton.
Grey Owl, At Geronimo's Grave, **Coteau Books**, Regina.

Maria Campbell's books:
Halfbreed, **McClelland & Stewart Ltd.**, Toronto: The Canadian Publishers.
Stories of the Road Allowance People, **Theytus Books**, Penticton.

Introduction

This is a book about ten people who tell stories, and about the stories they tell.

But let me start with a short story of my own. This book – stories about our story keepers –started out as a television program. Once upon a time, as a journalist, I began to seek out and talk to some Aboriginal writers I admired, preparing material for a television series profiling Indigenous storytellers. Everyone loved the idea – who wouldn't want to spend time with some of the funniest, most articulate authors in Canada? The problem, as always in Canadian broadcasting, was funding. There wasn't enough of it.

But if there's one thing I learned in talking to the story keepers, it's this: stories WILL be told. They don't care about funding. So another opportunity presented itself. Ningwakwe Learning Press appeared and welcomed the opportunity to publish a book profiling Aboriginal writers. And the National Literacy Secretariat of HRSDC agreed to fund it. Like all the best stories – a happy ending.

"All Aboriginal people are storytellers", Maria Campbell told me. And she was right.

Meeting the storytellers profiled in these pages, talking to them and hearing their stories, has been a great experience. They are of different ages, men and women, from every corner of Canada. Some grew up in the bush, some in the city. Many struggled with the English language, or fought to keep their own language. They write songs, novels, radio documentaries, history, poems, children's stories, plays, essays, speeches, and jokes. Some are at the peak of long, distinguished careers; some are just beginning.

But their stories – the ones they write, and the ones they live - all share certain characteristics. A passionate belief in the power of words to heal, to wound, to create. Lives are shaped by the stories told by parents, grandparents, elders. A reverence for storytelling as a bridge between hearts, eras, and peoples. And most of all, a faith that stories are an indestructible vessel for bringing old wisdom to life in a new time.

Canada has always enjoyed more than its share of exceptional, award-winning writers. In many ways, the work of Aboriginal authors is the most Canadian of Canadian writing: and yet, for years, their work has been relegated to a literary reserve, the "Native Lit" shelves at the back of small bookstores. And a very small shelf it was: several of the authors profiled herein began writing when they went looking for books on their own history and culture, and found nothing. So they wrote.

Literature has always built bridges of understanding between individuals and between peoples. That on its own would be reason enough to seek out these featured authors. But there's a better reason to read them: they have written great books. Not just great "Aboriginal" literature, but great books; important, and exciting works that deserve a national and international audience.

And they're finding it. Canada and the world are beginning to realize what treasures were buried on that "Native Lit" shelf. The ten writers who shared their thoughts with me represent only a small fraction of the exciting new work being produced by our Indigenous authors. Tomson Highway, Michael Kusugak, Eden Robinson, Thomas King, Brian Maracle are no longer just "niche" writers.

To all of you who have read and loved these writers – and to those of you who will read and love them - thank you/miigwetch for taking the time to read **Story Keepers**. Join us in spreading the word about the extraordinary explosion of literary talent taking place within our Aboriginal community. I hope the discovery enriches your life and your spirit, as it has mine.

Acknowledgements

Every single person who worked on this book with me had the same hope: to spark an interest in Indigenous literature among Aboriginal students and readers, and to make them proud of their rich and varied cultures by introducing them to books that speak directly to their experiences.

I would like to thank, first and foremost, all the writers who took the time to sit down with me and tell me their stories. It was a privilege and a pleasure.

I would like to thank Ningwakwe Learning Press, especially Priscilla George and Bob Rice, without whom this project would have never come to life.

I would also like to acknowledge the enthusiastic support of the National Literacy Secretariat at Human Resources Skills Development Canada, and also the Ontario Arts Council, particularly Denise Bolduc, for encouragement and financial support of this project.

I would particularly like to thank Paul Seesequasis at the Canada Council for the Arts, Vic Linklater, Ron Gallant, Terry Rudden my meticulous editor, Tania Koenig, who worked tirelessly with me, and Jaime Koebel, who transcribed all the interviews.

And finally and most of all, thanks to Jerico, who was ever-patient with me through the trials and tribulations and nail-biting moments of this entire journey, especially during the months when the birth of our first son, Caleb, provided a counterpoint in our lives to the writing of this book.

There are countless others who have been enthusiastic supporters of **Story Keepers**, either in its present incarnation or in its earlier video existence. I can't list you all, but I can thank you. And I do.

Note: All quotes attributed to the authors in this book have been taken from interviews that the authors gave with Jennifer David in 2002 and 2003. Other quotes are from various other sources, as footnoted.

Photo Credits:

Cover photograph courtesy of the Provincial Museum of Alberta.

Richard Van Camp by Tim Atterton

Drew Hayden Taylor by McKenna Photography

Gregory Scofield by Kelly Speirs

Lee Maracle by Columpa C. Bobb

Louise Halfe by Don Denton

Basil Johnston by Charles Vanden Ouden Photography

Jeanette Armstrong by Greg Young-Ing

Armand Ruffo by Danielle Schaub

Photo by Tim Atterton

Richard Van Camp

With award winning novels, children's books, poetry, short stories, graphic novels, editorials, screenwriting, songwriting and radio dramas under his belt, it's safe to say that no one will ever accuse Richard Van Camp of resting on his laurels. Chosen as "the most promising young writer in Canada" by the Canadian Authors Association in 1997, Richard has lived up to the promise of his early success, and produced a body of work as powerful as it is diverse.

Richard was born and raised in Fort Smith, which he describes as "the most beautiful little town in the Northwest Territories... the gateway to Wood Buffalo Park, the pumpkin capital of the North, and the third best place in the whole world to see the northern lights. It's also officially quadrilingual with the Cree, Chipewyan, French and English language; so you can imagine the conversations in the bank line up."

Richard was the oldest of four boys, growing up in "a home filled with encouragement and a love for education". But his education came with a cost.

"My mother made a decision, out of love, that all her sons would learn French so we could go on to university and college. We were not taught Dogrib, my mother's tongue." So thanks to what he calls "some of the worst French teachers in human history", Richard graduated without being able to speak either French or Dogrib. "Now, when I travel, I get asked why I can't speak my mother's language, and why I can't speak French—I'm Canadian, aren't I? It's tragic, and I know I'm one of thousands of Aboriginal people who are in the same place; but I know this will change."

Like many of the writers profiled in this book, Richard sees a brighter future for today's youth. "It will be the younger generation who will grow up knowing their languages, because they'll learn of our ruthless history and how our trust was used against us. They'll learn about colonization, imperialism, disenfranchisement, the Indian Act, and everything else that went into trying to break us as a people. I can't wait!"

> "Growing up in the NWT, I loved to read. But I wasn't reading what I truly needed to read. I wasn't reading about the life I was living."

Richard developed an early passion for reading. But he was aware from an early age of the gap between the fiction he loved and the reality he experienced every day.

"Growing up in the NWT, I loved to read. But I wasn't reading what I truly needed to read. I wasn't reading about the life I was living. I wasn't reading about driving our snowmobiles to school, going to class for five hours, then driving across the highway to check my brother's trapline before going home to our log house that we built as a family, for a supper of caribou meat and potatoes."

In short, no one was writing about the northern life Richard lived and loved, a way of life he felt driven to describe as realistically as possible. "I wanted to talk about high school and the beauty of the North and the culture of the Dogrib and Northerners, but I also wanted to illuminate the social issues. Why are so many of us without our language? What, without the church, is truly our culture? Why is there so much addiction and silence? I wanted to use these as backdrops because I really feel that the North has come out of a shadow, the shadow of residential schools. And yet Northerners are so kind and generous with whatever they have. I wanted to capture that, too."

An idea for a story came to Richard while he was still in high school, a story about an outsider and a Dogrib youth. It was the seed of what would become his powerful first novel five years later. But even as characters and situations began to take shape, Richard didn't think of himself as a writer. In fact, he initially considered himself a pen artist. And then he noticed a change in his drawings.

"What happened was, I started to actually worry more about the title of my drawings than what I was drawing. The titles began to wrap around the page. Then the drawings started to get smaller and smaller until they just vanished. My craft evolved from what I was drawing to what I was writing."

After high school, Richard enrolled at Aurora College in Yellowknife, with the goal of becoming a Land Claims negotiator. It seems an unlikely step in the evolution of an artist, but Richard enjoyed it. The experience brought him into close contact with other northern Aboriginal people; it also helped him to reflect on and learn about his own culture, and enriched his sense of himself as a Dogrib.

It was in Yellowknife that Richard first began to write down his thoughts, his observations, and his feelings. One day Ron Klassen, one of his instructors, gave Richard some good advice.

"About eight months into the ten month course, Ron took me aside and said, 'Richard, you don't really belong here…you could stay here if you wanted to, but you're a writer. And you really need to be with others of your own kind."

Another watershed moment occurred when Richard read **Gatherings**, a collection of works published by students and writers affiliated with the Enow'kin Centre, an international Aboriginal writing program in Penticton, B.C.

"I took the book home and inhaled (the stories.) For the first time, I saw other Aboriginal people writing down their thoughts and feelings. And it was so good! Right away I had to know more."

Stirred by his reading of **Gatherings**, Richard investigated the writing program at the Enow'kin Centre, applied, and was accepted in 1992. It was a seminal experience in his development as an artist. "That was where I found my voice as a writer and as a storyteller. I learned to take the best from different artists, but ultimately to forge my own voice from all the great teachings."

Those teachings came from many sources. One of Richard's mentors was another student, a gifted Aboriginal writer named Lorne Simon, who died tragically before his first book was published. His death had a profound effect on Richard, who credits Lorne as an important influence on both his life and his writing. "I became a writer the day I heard he died. When I write now I feel him around me. We still talk, Lorne and I. I know he guides my hand. He taught me more about writing than any school. Writing is about feeling. It's about gut. It's raw. It's sexy. It's impact."[1]

Richard continued his studies at the University of Victoria. It was during his final year of university that his experiences – Yellowknife, the Enow'kin Centre, and the tragic death of Lorne Simon – finally led him to complete the story that had taken shape years before.

"Somewhere along the way a young character named Larry Sole came up to me and he whispered in my ear for five years, and he told me the most incredible things. And that's how I wrote **The Lesser Blessed**."

Called "provocative" and "powerful", **The Lesser Blessed** is the story of Larry Sole, a typical Dogrib teenager growing up in the NWT of the 1980s, finding

7

his way through a world of heavy metal music, raging hormones and cultural transition.

Larry's stepfather, Jed, a traditional trapper and hunter, tries to encourage Larry to seek out his culture, but Larry is uncomfortable.

> "Did you start taking drum lessons?" he asked me.
>
> "No," I said. "I don't know any instructors."
>
> "Well, what about the Friendship Centre? Just go and ask. They'll show you."
>
> "Naw, Jed. I don't know. It's not my thing."
>
> "Well, pardner, what about jigging? Didja learn how?"
>
> "No."
>
> "Dja try?"
>
> I shook my head.
>
> "Well, what's it gonna be? The fiddle or the drum? You gotta take a side. It's just like the old-timers say, 'How can you know where you're going, if you don't know where you've been?'"[2]

Larry feels more comfortable listening to Iron Maiden and pining over his one love, Juliet. No superlatives are adequate to describe her: Larry spends much of his time reflecting on her various delectable body parts, including her pure white face, her perfect teeth, and her "marvellous ass in her tight black pants". In the end, Larry gets his girl - but not without a good measure of teenage angst and adolescent betrayal.

Given that Richard set out to write a realistic novel about youth and life in the North, it's no surprise that sexuality is a major theme in **The Lesser Blessed**.

"I wanted a voice that cut through that wall of silence. And I love to get down and dirty and very raunchy with my work, because in the North, there's still a lot of shame, sexually. I want to betray this and bring back the celebration of sexuality, sensuality and the erotic."

Richard's love of music surfaces throughout his writing. In the words of his protagonist Larry Sole, "Every song is a beautiful forest to get lost in."[3] Richard refers to music as "...my medicine. It's always been that way for me. I think it's like that for Aboriginal peoples everywhere. Music is our medicine; we're people of the drum. I've always been a slave to good music. It's made me shameless in how beautiful I feel. It's made me feel so magnificent – it's brought good medicine for me and a level of light. I will listen to music when I write to get into a certain mood."

Several episodes in **The Lesser Blessed** record, with brutal honesty, scenes of violence, alcohol and solvent abuse. In one scene, Larry recalls a buried memory of his father assaulting his aunt, and his own brush with solvent sniffing to escape the memory.

"I tried to scream but I couldn't. When I surfaced, I was in the sniff shack with my cousins. I stunk of gasoline and my father's blood. My hands were sticky. It was in my hair. We were all sniffing and Franky had a nosebleed. He was staggering. There was red paint splashed on his shoes. He was crying. His father was punched out somewhere, bleeding daddy blood. My cousin Alex was crying, too, because we knew we had no one. No one to remember our names, no one to cry them out, no one to greet us naked in the snow, to mourn us in death, to feel us there, in our sacred place. We wept because we did not belong to anyone."[4]

> "You can train your whole life to be a writer but to be a published author it's like firing a bullet—it's something that you can never take back."

But the hard edges are tempered by passages of sensitivity and humour, and the book is suffused with an unmistakably real sense of time and place, capturing an engaging group of characters in a unique period of northern and Aboriginal life.

Publication of **The Lesser Blessed** changed Richard's life. He had originally written the book for himself; but when it was published, he found himself answering to his family, his friends, and occasionally even to strangers in the North for the harsh, unsparing honesty of his story. "You can train your whole life to be a writer but to be a published author it's like firing a bullet— it's something that you can never take back."

Word of the novel's success reached Europe, where, to Richard's surprise, it was translated in France and in Germany. The book went on to win the 2001 Jugendliteraturpreis, Germany's most prestigious national award for juvenile fiction in translation. It was a culmination that Richard says he could never have imagined.

But the successful young novelist was already exploring new fields. While working in a summer bush camp back in the NWT, Richard found himself engaged in a completely different kind of writing – this time, for television.

"There I was, carpeted with mosquitoes, bulldogs and black flies, shovelling out dog pens in the bush. And suddenly there's a phone call for me. It was Jordan Wheeler from **North of 60**, the television series. And he asked me if I'd like to write for the show."

Northern insects and dogpens couldn't compete with that offer. Richard was soon working as an intern on the set of the popular television series, bringing a northern and Dene perspective to the episodes. Although he enjoyed the opportunity, he was glad to return to his own work; writing for television was too much like "writing by committee."

Radio provided another opportunity for work in a new medium. In 1998, Richard was commissioned by the CBC to write a radio drama for their Festival of Fiction. "Mermaids" was broadcast nationally, and then published - first in an anthology called **Skins,** and then in a collection of Richard's short fiction, **Angel Wing Splash Pattern**.

At this point most writers would have paused for breath. But as **The Lesser Blessed** was being published, Richard was invited by a publisher to write a book for children. He had never written specifically for children before, but the challenge appealed to him; and there was one special piece of adult short fiction, a tale about a raven, that had always felt to Richard like a children's story. From that short piece came **A Man Called Raven**. Published in 1998 with illustrations by well-known Cree artist George Littlechild, it won a Wordcraft Circle of Native Writers award.

"The book meant the world to me", says Richard, "because it was really a way of honouring the Elders in Fort Smith." He had always regretted the barrier of language that separated him from his own grandparents, who spoke no English. But while volunteering as a Handi Bus driver in Fort Smith, he met six elders (Dora Torangeau, Irene Sanderson, Rosa Mercredi, Seraphine Evans, Helene Mandeville and Maria Brown) who "took me under their Cree and Chipewyan wings", and taught him. "Not only did I now have adopted grandmothers who could speak English - but they also told me very beautiful stories." **A Man Called Raven** incorporated elements of the stories Richard heard from his "grandmothers" and his mother, Rose Wah-shee; its central theme, familiar in traditional tales, is a warning about the terrible consequences of cruelty to animals.

In the story, two brothers are confronted by an elder after trying to hurt a raven cornered in their garage.

"You don't know this" but you were asking for a lot of trouble when you were beating on that raven", the elder tells the brothers. "Your parents told me that you have never gone out on the land. Well, maybe that explains your actions. But I want to tell you a story about a man who liked to hurt ravens."[5]

The brothers hear the tale of a bitter old man whose loneliness and anger lead him to practice cruelty against animals. Upon dying, he transforms into a raven, and plans to torment his former community. But he discovers to his shock that the community is grieving for him; and he becomes their beloved protector.

Richard enjoyed writing the book, and its success led the publisher to propose another children's book in collaboration with George Littlechild. Richard recalls being asked if he had any stories about horses. "I lied and said, 'Oh, I've got a million stories.' We never really had horses growing up because it was too cold and the mosquitoes got at the horses. I didn't ride my first horse until I met my wife. So after I told this little fib that I had a million stories about horses, I was told I had five days to give them a story!"

Under pressure of time, Richard came up with an inventive solution. He simply asked everyone he knew to answer the question, "*What's The Most Beautiful Thing You Know About Horses*?" And that question became both the title and the theme of his second children's book, which is now included in the Canadian Children's Book Centre's list of recommended books.

In 2002, Richard published *Angel Wing Splash Pattern,* a collection of what he says are his "finest short stories so far." They are modern stories of Dogrib people, alive with a sense of spirituality and redemption. Richard acknowledges the importance of oral storytelling and its influence on his writing in these stories. "The Dogrib, we were a very mobile nation. We always had to follow the caribou. I really believe that our heart is in our stories because they're mobile too. The art is in our beadwork that goes onto our moccasins and our clothing. I've never really heard anybody talk about that before— that our art became our stories and that our stories became our medicine."

> "The Dogrib, we were a very mobile nation. We always had to follow the caribou. I really believe that our heart is in our stories because they're mobile too."

Fire is a recurring image in *Angel Wing Splash Pattern*. The main character in "Mermaids" is Torchy, a pyromaniac who can't understand his own fascination with fire. In "Snow White Nothing for Miles", a Dogrib elder, Icabus, is cursed after setting fire to a sweat lodge set up by enterprising Crees. His reluctant apprentice, Morris, asks plaintively, "What is it with Dogrib and fire?"[6] To Richard, the significance of fire in his stories goes beyond the obvious northern need for warmth; it is a cleansing ritual, image redemption. "There were huge, sweeping epidemics of TB and influenza in the North…that must have been hell on earth for the people…some were so bad that the Dogribs had to burn everything with fire. That's how the Dogribs cleansed. As well, we put food in the fire to feed our ancestors and tobacco to make an offering. We call this 'Feeding the Fire.'"

The characters in many of Richard's short stories are quietly mourning the passage of their culture and tradition. In **Sky Burial**, Icabus, the Dogrib elder approaching death, decides to pass on his medicine to a young Cree girl who he sees in the mall with her adopted white mother; he knows he cannot pass it on to his own family. In a brief, stinging paragraph, Richard evokes the elder's pain and sense of loss.

> "To his right, a table away, sat a family of ruined Indians.
> They had all let themselves go. They fed on burgers, fries,
> shakes. The mother had cut her hair. The kids were
> pudgy. The man was soft. Where are the warriors? Icabus
> had been waiting for a nod or a sign of acknowledgment,
> but the Indians wouldn't meet his eyes. What's happened
> to us? he thought. What the hell has happened to all of
> us?"[9]

Although many of his characters have a pessimistic view of life and the future, Richard is an optimist. He recently completed his Master's degree at UBC, and is currently finishing several novels, writing short stories, and developing other children's books. He has co-written a screenplay for a short movie called **Promise Me**, and is a frequent contributor to various magazines, newspapers and periodicals, as well as a number of online publications.

And of course, there's always a new medium Richard is ready to explore. He's very interested in working in a format relatively unknown in Canada: the graphic or illustrated novel. "I think it's the most exciting genre. If you know me, you know I love art. That's what I really want to break into. I really want to do that: my writing and somebody else's art. I've been training my whole life to write those kinds of stories. And I will do that; it's just a matter of time."

Fuelling Richard's optimism and enthusiasm is his belief that Canadian Aboriginal writers are growing stronger. He sees himself as following a trail blazed by Aboriginal women like Jeannette Armstrong, Ruby Slipperjack and Lee Maracle, joining a new generation that includes writers like Gregory Scofield and Eden Robinson. And he's passionate about the future of Aboriginal literature in this country.

"The themes that we're all dealing with are very similar: identity, inheritance, family, residential schools. Finally, we're coming into the light again. They say that when you break a bone in your body and it's a clean break, when the body heals itself there's a ring where that bone was broken. When they dig you up 500 years from now, if they look at that bone, it will have become the strongest part of the body. That's how powerful we are, and that's how powerful our spirits are. And I really believe that we were broken with residential schools and our history of foster care. I believe that that broke us. It's this new generation and it's the love of our mothers, Elders and ancestors that made us stronger; and now there's no stopping us."

NOTES

Excerpts from Richard Van Camp's books appear courtesy of the following publishers:

Angel Wing Splash Pattern, Kegedonce Press.

The Lesser Blessed, Douglas and McIntyre

A Man Called Raven, Children's Book Press.

[1] Daniel David Moses and Terry Goldie, ed **An Anthology of Canadian Native Literature in English.** (Toronto: Oxford University Press, 1998) 524.

[2] Richard Van Camp, **The Lesser Blessed**. (Vancouver: Douglas and McIntyre, 1996) 68.

[3] Van Camp, **The Lesser Blessed,** 7.

[4] Van Camp, **The Lesser Blessed,** 79.

[5] Richard Van Camp, **A Man Called Raven** (San Francisco: Children's Book Press, 1997)

[6] Richard Van Camp, "Snow White Nothing for Miles," **Angel Wing Splash Pattern** (Cape Croker: Kegedonce Books, 2002) 56.

[7] "Sky Burial," **Angel Wing Splash Pattern**, 41.

Major Works by Richard Van Camp

A Man Called Raven. Children's Book Press, 1997.

Angel Wing Splash Pattern. Cape Croker: Kegedonce Press, 2002.

The Lesser Blessed. Vancouver: Douglas and McIntyre, 1996.

What's the Most Beautiful Thing You Know About Horses? San Francisco: Children's Book Press, 1998.

Radio Dramas with CBC Radio One - **Mermaids**, 1998, **Sky Burial,** 2002.

Spoken Word Poetry on CD - "the uranium leaking from port radium and rayrock mines is killing us" with Redwire Magazine and CD. (Vol.5 Issue 4 April-August 2003)

Screenplay - "**Promise Me**" co-written with Kent Williams and Jason Alexander of Neohaus Filmworks, 2003.

For more details on Richard and his works, see: www.richardvancamp.org

Drew Hayden Taylor

Inspired by comic books and horror stories, and against the advice of both family and teachers, Drew Hayden Taylor has managed to make a living as a playwright, columnist and prolific writer: a living that has taken him around the world, and earned him numerous awards.

Drew's literary career began before he was even able to read. "I remember my mother bringing home comic books. I loved comic books. I would look at the pictures and I actually have a conscious thought of looking through comic books at five years old thinking, 'Wow, next year I'll go to school and I'll be able to read them, and then it will be completely different.'"

After comic books came a voracious appetite for horror. "Even before Stephen King, I would read anything, and people would roll their eyes at me. I would read all kinds of pop fiction and things like Frankenstein, Planet of the Apes, Conan the Barbarian." Those early books taught Drew how to "write a good story economically" - a lesson that would later prove useful.

Born on the Curve Lake reserve in central Ontario, Drew grew up with his mother in a very close-knit community. "It was boring growing up on the reserve, but in retrospect it was safe. I climbed trees, went swimming in the lake, and being safe was never an issue. I had over 60 cousins, so it was a piece of cake."

He never knew his non-Native father, and to this day has no desire to know him. His father's legacy, however, forced Drew to confront the issue of identity and what it means to be Aboriginal – a theme he addresses in much of his writing. A self-described "blue-eyed Ojibway", Drew grew up with a unique insight into people's perceptions of Aboriginal people.

Drew was different from many of the other kids on the reserve because he was an avid reader. The idea of becoming a writer came naturally to him.

"I always thought it would be great to be able to create universes and characters, create reality and see what happens," he says. "I didn't know that much about writing, but I thought it was something that could be fun." Despite that early interest, Drew's career as a writer almost came to a premature end. He asked his English teacher if it was possible to make a living as a creative writer. "Not really", said the teacher. Drew abandoned the idea.

> "A self-described "blue-eyed Ojibway", Drew grew up with a unique insight into people's perceptions of Aboriginal people."

He tried his hand at journalism, writing an article about a local band election and submitting it to an Aboriginal newspaper. The article was never published, the newspaper went out of business, and Drew decided to become an astronomer instead.

"That dream came from all my reading. But do you know how much math you need to study astronomy? I knew I wasn't fit for it."

Drew then studied radio broadcasting at Seneca College in Toronto, and found work traveling across the country with a television documentary crew as a sound recorder. "I wasn't the best boom man," he acknowledges ruefully. But he did enjoy meeting and talking to many different people during his travels, and his experience became fodder for his later work.

After working for CBC radio and following a stint as a production assistant on the television series **Spirit Bay,** Drew was suddenly presented with the opportunity of a lifetime. "I was 24 years old and I was talking to the story producer for a show called the **Beachcombers**, asking her if they had ever had any Native scriptwriters on the show. Next thing I knew, I got a call from the **Beachcombers,** and they asked if I had the ability to write a script by myself. I had several story ideas and I just wrote them. One of them became a series finale for one of the seasons."

That pivotal opportunity was the beginning of Drew's writing career, and it led quickly to other scriptwriting jobs.

There's a strong element of serendipity in the evolution of Drew's work, such as his shift from TV scriptwriting to playwriting. "Tomson Highway was the artistic director at Native Earth Performing Arts and had just received a grant to create a playwright-in-residence program. Since there were virtually no Native playwrights, he offered me the job. I was disinterested but needed the money…I'm probably one of the only people around who actually went into the theatre for the money!"

This unlikely introduction to the stage gave Drew an appreciation and understanding of how the theatre works. As part of his residency, he was asked to write a play. His first effort was called **Up the Road**, which Drew says was way too long; he "took it into the back yard and buried it." That might have been the end of his playwriting career; but then came an introduction to theatre director Larry Lewis.

Lewis asked Drew to write the play that became his first critical success. It was called **Toronto at Dreamer's Rock**.

"I said to myself, I really like science fiction; and I was thinking about the concept of identity, what being Native means to different people, and how they look, and how they're brought up. I brought those two ideas together and ended up writing the play."

The play revolves around an Aboriginal youth named Rusty. While sitting on a spiritually significant outcropping called Dreamer's Rock, Rusty encounters one boy from the past and another from the future. The misunderstandings, confusion and heated debate between the three young people create an insightful and moving look at tradition, language, and what it means to be an Aboriginal person.

"This is a play that, technically, shouldn't work. First of all, it's one scene without breaks. Second, there is very little physical space on Dreamer's Rock. Third, it's a very issue-oriented, 'think-heavy' play. It's a group of teenagers sitting there fighting, laughing, crying, arguing."

But the play did work. It was published immediately, won the Chalmers Canadian Play award, and has toured schools across the country nearly continuously since it was first produced in 1990.

> "I remember sitting around with my aunts and uncles on a lazy day with my grandparents telling stories. Maybe not traditional stories with Nanabush, but they were great stories that had a beginning, middle and end."

A string of other successful plays followed, including **The Bootlegger Blues**, which won the Canadian Authors Association Literary Award, and its sequel **The Baby Blues,** winner of the University of Alaska Native Playwriting Contest.

"I remember sitting around with my aunts and uncles on a lazy day with my grandparents telling stories. Maybe not traditional stories with Nanabush, but they were great stories that had a beginning, middle and end."

What are the sources of Drew's talent as a playwright? In addition to his curiosity and his voracious consumption of pop fiction, Drew credits a natural ear for storytelling.

"You're using your voice, body and imagination. Other media, like being a novelist, mean you have to have a very good understanding of the English language…if you want to write for TV and film, you have to understand that medium. But theatre is so intrinsically close to storytelling that it's 'six inches to the left' of traditional storytelling."

A sense of humour also comes naturally to Drew. His unique blend of wit, irony and sarcasm is perhaps most evident in his articles for magazines and newspapers across the country. Three volumes of his collected columns have been published under the title **Funny, You don't Look Like One.** In the introduction to the first volume, Drew lays out his philosophy of identity, and sets the stage for his recurrent theme of living with mixed-blood ancestry.

"I've spent too many years explaining who and what I am repeatedly. So as of this moment, I officially secede from both races. I plan to start my own separate nation. Because I am half Ojibway and half Caucasian, we will be called the Occasions. And of course, since I'm founding the new nation, I will be a Special Occasion."[1]

Nothing evokes Drew's sardonic wit as quickly as hypocrisy, whether within government or among well-meaning but ignorant supporters of Aboriginal causes. After hearing a lecture from a vegetarian denigrating the eating of meat and implying that meat "destroys the body rather than builds it up", and that humans were "not meant to be carnivores," Drew points out the reality of Aboriginal history. "[If] Nature has not made us carnivores, tell that to all the Aboriginal tribes of North America, especially the northern nations, whose diet consists mostly of meat. I'd like to see a vegetarian try and dig up a potato in three feet of snow. The Plains Indians survived almost totally on a diet of buffalo meat and they were amongst the strongest, healthiest people on the continent."[2]

> "You're using your voice, body and imagination [in theatre]. Other media, like being a novelist, mean you have to have a very good understanding of the English language…but theatre is so intrinsically close to storytelling that it's 'six inches to the left' of traditional storytelling."

Any topic, from erotica to government bureaucracy to German tourists to Hollywood movies, is fair game for Drew's columns. Most people who read his articles find something to relate to: his three essay collections have the broadest appeal of all his work.

Humour is also a central element of his plays, something that was not Drew's original intention. "When I wrote **Toronto at Dreamer's Rock,** I didn't think it was very funny, but everyone said it was so funny…then, before I wrote **Bootlegger Blues**, I met two Native women coming up to me after a play saying, 'you know, I'm not going to go to any more Native plays because I'm tired of being depressed." Thanks to those observations, and with the encouragement of Larry Lewis, Drew wrote **Bootlegger Blues** as a comedy. It was the summer of 1990, a difficult time to be experimenting with Native humour.

"We'd be rehearsing the play, then go home and watch the Oka crisis on the news. It was depressing, and we thought the play would be a huge bomb."

Instead, the play became an instant hit, winning awards and impressing audiences across the country. **Bootlegger Blues** is essentially a romantic comedy, built around three interwoven stories. A church-going woman finds herself stuck with 143 cases of beer that she begins to bootleg on the reserve, much to the chagrin of her police officer son. This same son falls in love with a woman he thinks is his cousin; then his sister runs off with a young pow wow dancer, leaving behind her straight-laced husband.

Bootlegger Blues earned Drew the best review of his life; an Elder, after seeing the play, approached him and told him," Thanks! You kind of made me homesick!'"

Humour plays a big part in the sequel to **Bootlegger Blues**. In his introduction to **The Baby Blues**, Drew says the play is "designed as a way of applauding the humour and merriment that exists in today's Native community. After many decades of seeing the media highlight the image of the "tragic" or "stoic" Indian, I felt Native people, and consequently non-Native people, were being given a raw deal. I know far more laughing First Nations people than depressed ones. I felt this disproportionate representation had to be addressed."[3]

> "After many decades of seeing the media highlight the image of the "tragic" or "stoic" Indian, I felt Native people, and consequently non-Native people, were being given a raw deal. I know far more laughing First Nations people than depressed ones."

The play introduces us to an enthusiastic young White woman named Summer, drawn to a local pow wow to "see the dancing, feel the power of the drum, and breathe in the essence of being Native." Her encounter with a thoroughly modern Aboriginal man named Skunk is humorous and insightful. When he notices she is obviously not an Aboriginal person, the following conversation ensues:

> SUMMER: No, I admit it, I was raised as a member of the oppressive white majority that is responsible for the unfortunate economic and social conditions your people live in. But really, deep, deep down inside, I'm a good person. Really I am! That's why I took this Native Studies class. Don't blame me for what they have done. I want to atone for their sins."
>
> SKUNK: Right. Well, okay, whatever turns your crank.
>
> SUMMER: But wait, you didn't let me finish. I am also taking Native Studies because, though I have not been skilled in the ways of the Elders, I do consider myself a part of the great aboriginal collective.
>
> SKUNK: You do?

SUMMER: For though I stand before you, Caucasian in
appearance, I want you, as my Native brother to know I too
carry the blood of your ancestors in my veins.

SKUNK: Nooooo!!

SUMMER: It's the truth. I only found out last year. In our
family archives, I found evidence that my great-great-
grandmother, Donna Seymour—may her spirit walk with
the Grandmothers—was one-quarter Native.

SKUNK: You're kidding!

SUMMER: No, but I haven't yet found out what particular
Nation she belonged to—or I for that matter—but we are
all brothers and sisters in the fight against the white
oppressor.

SKUNK: If your great-great-grandmother was one-quarter,
that would make you...

SUMMER: I am proud to say one-sixty-fourth. And proud
of every aboriginal cell in my body. Can you see it in my
features?

SKUNK: Ah yeah, yeah, right around your...um, nostrils.

SUMMER: You see it too!! I keep telling people. The
genes are too strong to be diluted.

SKUNK: Party on, Pocahontas.[4]

Drew skilfully exposes and plays upon Aboriginal and non-Aboriginal
stereotypes, but always gently and without malice. His work invites audience
members to laugh at their own prejudices and gain insight into the reality of
Aboriginal life. It is akin to teasing, a kind of humour seen in indigenous
communities around the world.

"There's an Elder from the Blood tribe who said, 'Humour is the WD40 of
healing.' I think humour was our form of storytelling. Over the years of having
our language and culture taken away and destroyed...I think our intrinsic
humour has survived. I've been to a lot of places in Canada and in every
Native community I've been to, I've always been greeted by a smile and a joke
and usually a laugh."

Humour has always helped Aboriginal people cope with difficult or tragic
situations. That aspect of the culture is reflected in the play **Someday,** which
Drew wrote in 1991. A play about fear, longing and the tragedy of broken
families, it describes the forcible removal of children from Aboriginal homes
and their placement in foster homes or residential schools. **Someday** tells the
story of one woman who was forced to give up her infant daughter, and is

about to meet her nearly 35 years later.

"There is humour in this play- but for some reason, it's more organic humour. It's much more realistic…I've been to funerals in my community where people are still telling jokes, but it is jokes in pain. I already knew the power of humour - but with **Someday,** I also learned the power of tears."

After discovering that her long-lost daughter Grace is about to make a visit to the reserve, Anne begins to panic. She tries to solicit advice from Barb, her second daughter, and from her boyfriend Rodney.

> ANNE: I've got to buy groceries. She'll probably be half-starved to death. What should I cook? She's probably used to white food. I sure can't cook her Indian food then. What do white people eat, Rodney?
>
> RODNEY: Stuff like whole wheat and yogurt.
>
> ANNE: I gotta remember to get some of that stuff. Whole wheat and yogurt. Oh, and the tree. The Christmas tree. Will your brother lend us the car again, do you think? Then we can be a real family. We can all decorate the tree together like they do in the movies. Get us a nice tree, Rodney.[5]

The final meeting between mother and daughter is bittersweet. When Grace discovers she was removed from her home by the Children's Aid Society because of a misunderstanding, she is overwhelmed and says she cannot stay.

> RODNEY: You're leaving? Now? They have all sorts of things planned for you.
>
> JANICE: I know. And I hate to disappoint them, but I do have other commitments. [My family] is having a dinner tonight. I have to be there.
>
> RODNEY: But what about Anne and Barb? It's not supposed to end this way. This should be a happy movie like **It's a Wonderful Life.**
>
> JANICE: Don't tell me about movies. I'm an entertainment lawyer. Movies are my life. Ironic, isn't it?
>
> Rodney looks up and sees the silhouettes of the two women in the window.
>
> RODNEY: Grace…
>
> JANICE: Please call me Janice.

RODNEY: Why did you come all the way out here, Janice?

JANICE: Curiosity. There were some things I had to see and know. Both have been accomplished. It's time to go home.

RODNEY: Anne thinks this is your home.

JANICE: A couple of photographs, some tea, and a pair of moccasins don't make a home or a family. My family's waiting for me in London.[6]

The story was an important one for Drew. Few Canadians know how many Aboriginal children were taken from their families, or understand how these separations devastated individuals and communities.

The success of the play led Drew to write a sequel, which tells Grace and Janice's story.

"**Someday** showed that you can't overcome 35 years in one hour. All things important and necessary take time. Repatriation, reunification, whatever you want to call it, takes commitment and resolve. And the road is not always smooth…it was time for Janice to have her day and face her demons."[7]

Only Drunks and Children Tell the Truth explores the difficulty that adopted or fostered children have in re-claiming or re-discovering their heritage and birth families.

The play went on to win the Dora Mavor Moore Award. In her comment on the play, Aboriginal writer Lee Maracle wrote: "the magic of good writing…is to create the dramas of ordinary peoples' lives, to unfold them, and to keep the social conditions from which they arise solidly buried underneath in a way that jostles up the characters you have created."[8]

It is this ability to find and create drama in ordinary people's lives, or, as Drew calls it, "kitchen-sink drama," that keeps him passionate about his work.

"Kitchen sink drama simply means realism. This is what I write. I tried to be less realistic but I have trouble with that…I live in the real world and I have fun. I want to try to make it interesting."

Of all the plays he has written, **The Girl Who Loved Her Horses** is Drew's favourite. It tells the story of a young, abused girl who is befriended by a family. She is encouraged by the mother of the family to draw on the kitchen walls. The little girl draws a horse, which soon takes on a life of its own and brings her joy and comfort.

"This story is loosely based on a true story and it's my favourite because it is sad and pathetic. But it shows the power of art and of imagination. When I wrote it, I knew the horse would move but this was very difficult to produce…I enjoyed it because there was a lot of artistic exploration going on."

After producing nine plays, short stories, television dramas and countless articles, Drew would like to write a novel. His biggest challenge is having "so many ideas, so little time." He continues to read omnivorously, and cites his reading as his greatest source of insight and inspiration.

"Reading has just opened up worlds for me. You don't necessarily have to read "high literature" to find a good story...I read and store information that I can draw upon for my books...then I just write, write, write because it's like a muscle that needs to be used. It needs practice."

> "Kitchen sink drama simply means realism. This is what I write. I tried to be less realistic but I have trouble with that...I live in the real world and I have fun."

NOTES

Excerpts from Drew Hayden Taylor's books have been quoted with permission of the following publishers:

Baby Blues and **Only Drunks and Children Tell the Truth**—Talonbooks

Funny You Don't Look Like One—Theytus Books, Penticton.

Someday—Fifth House Ltd., Calgary.

[1] Drew Hayden Taylor, "Introduction," *Funny, You Don't Look Like One*. (Penticton, BC: Theytus Books, 1998) 8.

[2] Taylor, *Funny, You Don't Look Like One* 50.

[3] Drew Hayden Taylor, *The Baby Blues*, (Burnaby, BC: Talon Books, 1999) 7.

[4] Drew Hayden Taylor, *Someday*, (Saskatoon: Fifth House Publishers, 1993) 14.

[5] Taylor, *Someday* 78-79.

[6] Drew Hayden Taylor, "Introduction," *Only Drunks and Children Tell the Truth*., (Burnaby, BC: Talonbooks, 1998) 12.

[7] Taylor, *Only Drunks and Children Tell the Truth* 66.

Major Works by Drew Hayden Taylor

alterNatives. Vancouver: Talonbooks, 2000.

The Baby Blues. Burnaby: Talonbooks, 1999.

The Boy in the Treehouse and Girl Who Loved Her Horses. Vancouver: Talonbooks, 2000.

The Bootlegger Blues. Saskatoon: Fifth House, 1991.

The Buz'Gem Blues. Vancouver: Talonbooks, 2002.

Fearless Warriors. Burnaby: Talonbooks, 1998.

Funny, You Don't Look Like One. Penticton: Theytus Books, 1998.

Furious Adventures of a Blue-Eyed Ojibway: Funny, You Don't Look Like One, Two, Three. Penticton: Theytus Books, 2002.

Further Adventures of a Blue-Eyed Ojibway: Funny, You Don't Look Like One Two. Penticton: Theytus Books, 1999.

Only Drunks and Children Tell the Truth. Burnaby: Talonbooks, 1998.

Someday. Saskatoon: Fifth House, 1993.

Toronto at Dreamer's Rock and Education is our Right. Saskatoon: Fifth House, 1990.

Ruby Slipperjack

The land is a silent character in the works of Ruby Slipperjack, a presence that shapes and gives meaning to the others who people her novels and short stories. Her fiction is alive with a deeply felt sense of place, and with relationships that links her characters – and their author - to the land.

"[The land] is like the air we breathe…the land holds our history. Everything about our family happened on that land and every spot of land has a story."

Stories are the land's memories. And those memories, those stories, have been part of Ruby's imagination ever since she was a small girl.

> "The land is like the air we breathe...the land holds our history. Everything about our family happened on that land, and every spot of land has a story."

Born in a remote region of northwestern Ontario, Ruby Slipperjack was raised in a small cabin with her family – her father and mother, two brothers, five sisters, and assorted relatives. She remembers hunting and trapping by dogsled with her father, learning from her mother to tan and sew hides, to make fish nets to fish and to hunt. And she remembers the sound of wolves.

"They would yap and bark and howl across the lake, and at night we could hear them. The whole pack would run right across the lake…my mother would bang her pots together (to send them away.)"

Those wolves aren't Ruby's only canine memory. Her father had built a long house with individual compartments for the family's many dogs – a special and inviting place for a child. "I used to crawl in there. It was nice and cozy; it had pine branches in there to keep the dogs warm. It's one of my earliest memories."

When Ruby was seven years old, her family moved closer to the railway line so that she and her siblings could attend day school. She had never spoken English before in her life; her first day of school was also her introduction to another culture, tradition and language.

"I remember one teacher, he was trying to get us motivated to sing at Christmas. We didn't know anything about Christmas, and all of a sudden he wanted us to sing about it. 'Dashing through the snow, in a one-horse open sleigh…' It was pretty boring. So the boys started singing really loudly in Cree with words that sounded like 'dashing through the snow' but they were really saying 'there's crap in my pants.' Here they were singing, and the teacher can't figure out what he did to get these kids motivated to start singing so loud!"

> I remember the loneliness. I was so homesick. I grew up in a family where someone was telling stories all the time.

The day school held many good memories for Ruby. "We teased each other all the time!" But when she had to attend residential school, it was a different story. To a young woman raised in a tight-knit, large and social family, the solitude was difficult.

"I remember the loneliness. I was so homesick. I grew up in a family where someone was telling stories all the time. There was always a voice going, talking and telling stories."

Her solitude, however, was the catalyst that led Ruby to begin writing.

"I found myself in isolation with no one to tell my stories to - so I started writing them down."

Ruby's early stories were about animals, mythical little people, life on the land - themes she calls "just homesick kid stuff." They weren't intended for anyone else's eyes. Every summer she'd return home, take her bundle of stories to the woodstove – and burn them. And every fall, she'd go back to school, and begin writing a new year's worth of stories.

Ruby's fiction gives readers the sense of an Ojibway heart speaking with an English tongue. That unique voice began to take shape while she was still learning to read and write in English. "I was writing in English but my language in my head was Ojibway. It was natural to think in Ojibway and then write it down in English. I probably started translating when I was 12 years old."

Ruby also remembers illustrating some of those early, "homesick kid" stories. She has always enjoyed painting as a way to evoke her life in the bush.

"Whenever I went home in the summer, I had to soak it all in because it had to last me another year. I remember the sunset, and when it hit the leaves, the colour of the leaves on the tree. We didn't have cameras at the time, and I'd have to paint from memory." Ruby continues to paint to this day, and in fact provided the cover illustrations for two of her books.

Upon graduating from high school, Ruby set her sights on university. Her guidance counselor, however, didn't feel that was appropriate. "The counselor laughed and said that Indian girls don't go to university. He said there was a secretarial position open at Indian Affairs. So that's where I went and became a secretary."

It wasn't a happy experience. Ruby didn't like being a secretary, and she didn't like Toronto. After some time in the city, Ruby moved back to northern Ontario. While back home, she had an opportunity to teach adult education and she decided that she enjoyed teaching.

Ruby married, and began to raise small children at home. And she continued to write – and burn - her stories. Then, in a relocation fortunate for both Ruby and her future readership, Ruby moved to Prince Albert, Saskatchewan. Her new house had neither a fireplace nor a woodstove. She began to store her writing in boxes, where over the months segments of a novel about a young Ojibway girl "… just piled up, chapter after chapter."

Many of the authors profiled in this book were set on their path as writers by chance. In Ruby's case, it was a TV interview with a budding Aboriginal publisher that transformed Ruby's boxes of paper into her first published work. "I was watching TV one time and there was this Native woman saying that she was starting a Native publications company. It was Beatrice Culleton, a well-known Aboriginal writer herself. She was asking people if they had any stories to send to her." Intrigued, Ruby contacted her.

"I said I had some children's stories. She said, 'what I'm really interested in is a novel', and she asked me if I had a manuscript. Manuscript? I had my mountain of paper. I never thought of it as a manuscript. I said, 'I have a story, but I don't have an ending!' "

With some coaxing from Beatrice Culleton, Ruby found the ending she needed; *Honour the Sun*, her first novel, was published in 1987.

> "All the years of burning stories - I never wanted anyone to see them, and here they were, out there for everyone to see. I remember a panic feeling!"

The realization that she was now a published author didn't hit home until Ruby received the final publication in the mail. "One day, ten free copies arrived. I was looking at this. I wanted to crawl under the table. All the years of burning stories - I never wanted anyone to see them, and here they were, out there for everyone to see. I remember a panic feeling!"

Honour the Sun is a collection of diary entries by a young Ojibway girl nicknamed "the Owl". She records her life, her thoughts and her feelings over a period of years, as innocence becomes bittersweet adolescence and her family struggles to adapt to modern life.

The book is a rich, loving evocation of the sights and sounds of life in the bush.

> "I run as fast as I can through my shortcut home. The dry brown leaves crackle and swish under my feet. The air is crisp and cool. A flood of joy fills me as I dash into the clearing. Our cabin door is open: smoke is coming up in blue wisps and I hear voices and laughter." [1]

But warm memories of life on the land slowly give way to encroaching modernity. One by one, the Owl's brothers and sisters move away. One is taken to a sanatorium to be treated for tuberculosis; others leave to get work in distant lumber camps, or simply to move into town. Echoing the experience of Ruby's own childhood, families are forced to abandon their bush camps and traplines and move closer to the railway lines and the Indian Day Schools, a movement Ruby calls "forced relocation." With increased contact came the devastating effects of alcohol, chronicled in **Honour the Sun** in chilling scenes of children hiding in corners while drunken men break down doors looking for fights. After one such incident, in the middle of winter, the children are forced to go back to sleep with a broken door hanging on its hinges.

> "I jump down from my top bunk and stand shivering by the stove, holding out my hands to the heat. When I look at the door I feel like crying. I wish I were big, very big and strong: I'd squeeze that hateful man like a piece of cloth wrung out to dry and then I'd...I can feel warm tears running down my cheeks. No, I won't cry." [2]

Ruby wanted her story to be accurate, even if her honesty made the book more difficult to read – and write.

"I made no effort to shade things and I didn't temper or eliminate some of the 'bad' things that went on in communities." Her goal was to paint a picture of the life she knew. "I wanted to talk about the communities along the CNR mainline, since there was never any mention of them in any of the stories and literature of the time. Native literature in particular spoke only of urban or reserve life - if there was anything at all. I knew about life along the CNR mainline - and I wrote what I knew about."

Despite Ruby's initial panic, the book was well received and favorably reviewed. Still in print after more than fifteen years, **Honour the Sun** continues to sell, and is now included in the curriculum of many school districts. It is a coming of age story most young people can relate to.

"I'm not surprised people get something out of it," Ruby says. "It's the story of my life. We were all children at one point."

Now a published author, Ruby decided to pursue the education that her guidance counselor had declared "inappropriate". The former Indian Affairs secretary completed a BA, then a Bachelors of Education, and finally a Masters of Education from Lakehead University in Thunder Bay. Pursuing her studies required many sacrifices, especially in her family life. But Ruby had many more stories to tell; and in 1992, she published **Silent Words**, her second novel.

It's a book about the adventures of Danny, a young Ojibway boy who runs away from home, and is sheltered and taught on his journey by many different people. Through these encounters Danny, raised without knowing traditional ways, learns to respect nature, and to survive in the bush. He also learns the importance of silence, of knowing when to ask questions and when to be quiet and learn. In one scene, Mr. Old Indian finishes telling Danny a story. Bursting with questions, Danny manages to restrain himself, and simply ponders what the old man has said.

> I heaved a big sigh and noticed the old lady's black eyes on me from the table. I shrugged hopelessly and she smiled and looked away. I just did it! I mean talking not with words but by actions. I remembered my second day here, the old man had looked at the old woman, then at me. The old woman smiled and said, " 'e say you talk too much."

This idea of non-verbal communication or 'silent words' is a key concept in Ojibway, and other Aboriginal cultures.

> I had looked at the old man and said, "What? I didn't hear him say anything.

> "No," she said. "Use your eyes an feel inside you wat da udder is feelin. Dat way, dere is no need for words. Your ears are for 'earing all da udder things 'round you."[3]

This idea of non-verbal communication or 'silent words' is a key concept in Ojibway, and other Aboriginal cultures. When Ruby teaches from one of her books, she says she finds that Aboriginal students will intuitively understand unspoken interactions between characters that non-Aboriginal students sometimes miss. "An Aboriginal person will catch the non-verbal stuff, and will know what just happened in between...even though they're not aware that they're interpreting the things that aren't written."

Much of the inspiration for Ruby's writing comes from the many stories she heard as a child. Ojibway children grow up with tales of the great trickster, Weesquachak. Like stories of Raven, Coyote and other tricksters, these are tales of mischief, adventure and humour; but they also embody and express deep and complex cultural values, and teach valuable lessons about life. In

Weesquachak and the Lost Ones published in 2000, Ruby decided to introduce Weesquachak into a contemporary setting and see what would happen.

"Weesquachak comes walking along the beach. Nobody talks about him anymore; the people have forgotten about him. He sees two young people (who had been arranged to be married) and he decides to see what he can do."

> "They forgot about me. Their children have never even heard of me. The adults don't remember anymore. The old ones have no one to listen but I...I will not be forgotten! I will make them know that I still exist, I will make them get to know me again. I exist. I am here, always have been—right among them. Now, I've been watching this girl. She comes and goes and doesn't seem to know what she is supposed to do. She seems lost..." [4]

Ruby's story explores what the traditional trickster would do in a modern situation and a modern relationship. "So instead of trying to get these two people together, Weesquachak says he wants this girl for himself. Then they go through these adventures. Weesquachak is in there, causing miscommunications. They're all mixed up and they don't know who they are. Weesquachak is playing tricks; but sooner or later, we all know that he does something good, and he manages to get them together," says Ruby.

The main character, Janine, is struggling to find a balance between city life and her deep-rooted sensibilities. Her intended husband is a traditional hunter and trapper, and their relationship reflects the distance between old and new, between the city and the land. It is a conflict that is part of many Aboriginal lives, including Ruby's; she wrote ***Weesquachak and the Lost Ones,*** in part, to examine the tension between those different ways of living.

"How I am in the city is not how I would be growing up back home. Many students understand, 'hey, I've been there'. I just remind students to find a parallel between my books and their lives. You know that you're different when you go home and it's not the community that has changed—it's you."

Ruby continued to explore the struggle to find a life between the contemporary and traditional worlds in her next book, ***Little Voice***, a story for young readers.

"How I am in the city is not how I would be growing up back home. I just remind students to find a parallel between my books and their lives."

The main character, a young girl named Ray, is called Naens ("Little Voice") by her grandmother. She struggles to adjust to life in school, copes with the death of her father, and faces discrimination from her classmates. Through it all, Ray longs to be with her grandmother, a source of both love and deep learning.

(Grandma) leaned over closer to me and her black eyes
bore into mine as she said with great authority, "Naens,
you must now come forward with your voice or someone
else will take it away from you who is not supposed to
have it!"

That alarmed me. "What do you mean?" I asked.

She smiled and whispered, "You know very well that if we
have the knowledge and the skill to do something and do
not do it, there will be someone else that will do it...don't
you? They will take and run off with the knowledge of
Naens, because she could not speak to say it was hers." [5]

In **Little Voice**, Ray loves learning in any form. She is pulled between the
knowledge she acquires at school and the wisdom taught by her grandmother.
In the end, Ray comes to understand her obligation to the teachings of her
elders and her Ojibway traditions. She decides to follow in the footsteps of
her medicine-woman grandmother.

The story of Ray's struggle and decision depicts the challenge facing many
Aboriginal people, and especially youth. The theme of **Little Voice** – the
importance of tradition, and the affirmation of its value in the face of modern
life – is a central message that emerges in all of Ruby's books, and one that
she intends to explore further in her upcoming work.

Ruby has several books in progress, including a "fun novel", and a more serious
work built around the day-to-day life of Aboriginal people during the fur
trade era. She enjoys her work as the Chair of the Department of Indigenous
Learning at Lakehead University, continues to teach, and is completing a PhD.

These days Ruby is more likely to be found camping with her family than
living on a northern Ontario trapline; but her experience and knowledge of
the land remains the most important thing in her life and her work.

"What I find most precious are the things I learned before I went to school.
The language, the writing, syllabics, all the cultural knowledge that I have -
I've never forgotten. So, understanding life on the land and what goes on in
the trapline, I'll never forget. All the things they once told us to forget, the
knowledge they once called 'useless'–that's what has become most precious."

NOTES

Excerpts from Ruby Slipperjack's books have been quoted with permission by the following publishers:

Honour the Sun—Pemmican Publications
Silent Words—Fifth House Ltd., Calgary.
Weesquachak and the Lost Ones—Theytus books, Penticton.
Little Voice—Coutou Books.

[1] Ruby Slipperjack, *Honour the Sun* (Winnipeg: Pemmican Publications, 1987) 94.

[2] Ruby Slipperjack, *Honour the Sun*, 100-101.

[3] Ruby Slipperjack, *Silent Words*. (Saskatoon: Fifth House Publishers, 1992) 60.

[4] Ruby Slipperjack, *Weesquachak and the Lost Ones* (Penticton: Theytus Books, 2000) 7.

[5] Ruby Slipperjack, *Little Voice*. (Regina: Coutou Books, 2001) 13.

Major Works by Ruby Slipperjack

Honour the Sun. Winnipeg: Pemmican Publications Inc., 1987.

Little Voice. Regina, Coteau Books, 2001.

Silent Words. Saskatoon: Fifth House Publishers, 1992.

Weesquachak and the Lost Ones. Penticton: Theytus Books, 2000.

Gregory Scofield

"This is my story of survival and acceptance, of myself and my widening family. I write it for all of you who have survived and for those of you struggling to survive. Had it not been for the books I read as a teenager, I am sure I would not be at this place, today. Those very writers, people like Margaret Laurence, Maria Campbell, and Beatrice Culleton, made me want to write. They brought my mind and spirit to life. They gave me a sense of something larger than myself, something more profound than pain, fear and anger. They led me to a place of belonging, a permanent home where I have found a voice to speak with."[1]

And so Gregory Scofield begins his autobiography, **Thunder Through My Veins**, an intimate and frequently painful account of a young man's search for identity, meaning and belonging. He was only thirty-three when the book was published, an age when most are just beginning to settle into their life's path. But Gregory had already done more living than most, and he felt his story was one that others should hear.

"When writing **Thunder Through My Veins**, I was very conscious because I realized I would have given my eyeteeth in school to be able to go through the library and be able to pick out a book that I thought looked interesting and that I could relate to...[stories] about youth who are struggling with issues of belonging and acceptance."[2]

The importance of a sense of belonging – or its absence – has haunted Gregory since his childhood. Born in Maple Ridge, British Columbia, he spent his early years in northern Saskatchewan, northern Manitoba and the Yukon. He moved from community to community, first with his mother, Dorothy Scofield, and her husband: then, after his mother became too ill, with a series of foster families. His mother eventually regained her child, but she remained crippled by ill health and alcohol.

> *"I would have given my eyeteeth in school to be able to go through the library and be able to pick out a book that I thought looked interesting and that I could relate to...[stories about youth who are struggling with issues of belonging and acceptance."*

It was during this period, when he was seven years old, that Gregory met an older Cree woman, a neighbour named Georgina Houle Young. "Aunt Georgie's" friendship and support gave Gregory an emotional focus – and so did her recognition of his Aboriginal identity. In **Thunder Through My Veins** he describes their first meeting, when she immediately identifies him as Métis.

"Hmm," she began, bending down to examine my face. "You got grey eyes and light hair, but you also got a big nose, high cheekbones, and big fat lips." I felt my face going red and she started to laugh. "I tink you must be an *Awp-pee-tow-koosan*, like me," she concluded. "I see it, too, in your mama."

"What's that?"

"Dat's a half-breed. Half dis and half dat."

"Half what?" I asked, afraid of the answer.

"You know, half devil and half angel," she teased.

"I don't think so," I politely answered. "I think I'm a great chief like Sitting Bull and Red Cloud."

"Is dat so!" she called out, looking at me closely, a smile breaking across her lips. "Oh, yes, now I can see it."

I sat back proudly on the couch and dug into the milk and cookies, pondering what she had just said about being a half-breed.[3]

Métis heritage was never something his mother talked much about. His grandfather had kept his Aboriginal ancestry secret from his wife: partly because of the stigma associated with being Métis, and partly to shield his daughters, including Gregory's mother, from racism and discrimination.

"Perhaps, for Grandpa, it was the only way to try to guarantee them fairness and equality. And yet the price of his silence, the denial of his heritage, has left hundreds of unanswered questions and, I strongly believe, deeply affected each generation of my family. Little did I know that one day his silence would become the catalyst for my own self-acceptance, love, artistic expression, and ultimately, survival."[4]

Gregory explores Métis heritage and survival in a number of his poems, moving from the personal to the political, probing the deep and complex links between race, culture, and identity. He is acutely conscious of himself as a gay, Métis man; but he will not allow the colour of his skin or his sexual orientation to limit who he should or should not be.

> **"As soon as I was able to shrug off the clothes that other people were trying to make me wear and I started stepping into my own clothes, I was able to bring these two halves together and become a whole individual."**

"As soon as I was able to shrug off the clothes that other people were trying to make me wear and I started stepping into my own clothes, I was able to bring these two halves together, if you will, and become a whole individual. Culturally, it's who I am; and I was able to start celebrating other aspects of who I am as an individual."

Like many of the writers profiled in this book, Gregory was a creative child. "From a really young age, around 10 or 11, I remember writing little poems or stories, and it was my imaginary world. I tried to put down what was going on in the moment." As he grew older, he accumulated boxes of stories and poems he had written. Occasionally he'd burn them or simply throw them away. Both their creation and their destruction were cathartic.

"It was easy to rip them up and throw them away. I was completely disassociated with the feelings and emotions, the things I was struggling through with my poetry."[5]

In his early 20s Gregory began to show his poems to a few trusted readers, many of whom urged him to publish. It was not an idea he had ever considered.

"I never thought about writing as a career. I didn't know any writers, at least other Aboriginal writers. I had read other writers but I never thought of myself as one of them. I really didn't have any knowledge or direction. I had no idea that it could be a feasible career or that it would bring me so much healing."

He put his reservations aside, and quickly discovered that, for him, writing was, indeed, a feasible career. His first collection of poetry, **The Gathering: Stones for the Medicine Wheel,** was published in 1993, and won the 1994 Dorothy Livesay Poetry Prize. Reviewers praised its tough insights and energy. More modestly, Gregory describes it as "filled with the angst of a 26-year- old wanting to talk about what it was like being a 26-year-old Native man and what that culture was like."

It was soon followed by a second volume of poetry, **Native Canadiana: Songs from the Urban Rez**. The new poems reflect the squalor and rage in the lives he witnessed while working with youth at risk in downtown Vancouver. Many of his experiences there were difficult for him to deal with: poetry helped give shape and meaning to what he was seeing. "So many of our youth were coming down from remote communities…and I wanted to do something to try to empower them, to shed light on issues affecting them, so in the essence, the book became very political."

The book is full of strong, sometimes brutal writing. It angered some readers, particularly non-Aboriginal people, by pointing an unwavering finger at racist government policies and systemic discrimination.

> When the sun comes out
> The streets smell like piss
> Down here
> It doesn't matter what side
> Of the skids
> You're on
> You could be better than me
> I really don't give a damn
> If you think so
> Why not just say so
> I won't crumble
> Because you got a swollen-up head
> …
> How they got to pay taxes
> And we don't
> As if we said 500 years ago
> Put that in the treaty while you're at it
> Roll out that whiskey keg
> And don't forget to include
> An educational clause
> If we're going to be force-fed
> You glamorous take-over history
> Why not get paid to act
> The conquered part   the part where we say
> Hey, môniyâs I want my cheque
> Gimme my cheque right now
> You owe me
> For this left-over land
> We never sold, gave up, handed over…[6]

Understanding of Métis heritage, for Gregory, is synonymous with awareness of Métis history. He is appalled at how few Canadians – and, in fact, how few Métis – look beneath the surface of historical events to the deeper currents that run through their past.

"We really need to be educated. Not just about Louis Riel or the Northwest Rebellion. For example, we don't call it a rebellion; we call it a resistance. We need to ask - why was there a resistance? We need to look into historical facts like the Métis scrip, and how we were disenfranchised from our own homelands."

> "How do I act   I act without an Indian act
> Fact is I'm so exact about the facts
> I act up when I get told I don't count
> Because my act's not written
> So I don't get told who I am or where to go
> If I want to hang solo without my tribe
> Check out other rezless Indians
> No DIA director can pop me on a bus
> Send me home   homeless as I am
> I'm exact about my rights
> So exact in fact I act downright radical
> Though never hostile unless provoked
> …
> I'm not solely a First Nations act
> Or Canadian act
> But a mixed breed act
> Acting out for equality
> This is not some rebel halfbreed act
> I just scribbled down for revenge
> Besides
> I don't need to be hung
> For my mixed mouth blabbing
> How they used their act
> To cover up
> Dirty goings-on in our country.[7]

Gregory quit school in grade 10, though he returned years later as a mature student. He is essentially self-taught, and sees his poetry as a gift of the Creator. His voice as a writer came to him from many different places.

 "It's not that I chose poetry. It chose me…I never really sat down and thought about why I am a poet. I don't see myself as a poet. First, I'm a community worker and I do my community work with poetry…I am a story keeper. I'm a keeper of the stories from my history. I am a keeper of the medicines from those stories."

Poetry as medicine is an important theme in Gregory's third book of poetry, **Love Medicine and One Song**. Its lyrical, sensual eroticism is a surprising departure from the jagged, often angry poems of his earlier collections. Gregory calls this collection "my baby."

> "I'm a community worker and I do my community work with poetry…I am a story keeper. I'm a keeper of the stories from my history. I am a keeper of the medicines from those stories."

"I wanted a book about Aboriginal love poetry, not necessarily one about homoerotic poetry. I wanted a book that anybody could pick up and…realize that there was a whole universality about love and our bodies and our connections…In a kind of covert way, I wanted people to start seeing Aboriginal people in a whole different context."

> "I heat the stones
> between your legs,
> my mouth,
> the lodge where you come
> to sweat.
> I fast your lips
> Commune with spirits,
> Fly over berry bushes
> Hungering.
> I dance with sun,
> Float with clouds
> Your earth smell
> Deep in my nostrils,
> Wetting
> The tip of my tongue.
> I chant with frogs,
> Sing you to dreams,
> Bathe you in muskeg,
> Wrap you in juniper
> And sweet-pine.
> Nîcimos, for you
> I drink blessed water
> Chew the bitter roots
> So the medicine is sweet,
> The love, sacred.[8]

The poems interweave Cree phrases and natural imagery into a passionate celebration of union, both physical and spiritual, all deeply rooted in an Aboriginal sensibility. Gregory feels it is one of his most successful books, a " huge celebration of love and acceptance."

The publication of **Love Medicine and One Song,** Gregory's most life-affirming book to date, coincided with a particularly difficult period in his life. Many important people in his life died at this time, including his mother and his aunt. Once again, Gregory sought meaning and solace in his poetry, beginning a new series of what he calls "memory and grieving writing." As the poems took shape, he realized they all shared a common motif…his mother and his aunt.

"Well into writing the book, I realized it wasn't so much "about" them - but it was about all of our mothers, our aunties, and grandmothers. It was a celebration of Aboriginal women – a celebration of their strength, courage, determination, and power. At that point, I realized I wanted to publish a book about them. I wanted everybody to know them through the poems and to be able to walk in the homes they had created. I wanted the reader to come and sit at my aunty's table, have some tea and bannock and listen to her stories."

This cycle of love songs to Gregory's mother and his aunt was published under the title **I Knew Two Métis Women.** The poems mark another surprising shift of voice for Gregory. These are tender pieces; they evoke a sense of home and happy childhood memories.

> ...her guitar songs
> long after I fell to sleep,
> the smell of Pine-Sol,
> smoked moose hide, cinnamoned apples
>
> etching their way
> silently into my knowing,
> running deeper than the blood
> feeding my heart.[9]

The collection is filled with stories of laughter, love, hardship, and – hurtin' music. Gregory's family loved old-time country tunes and the likes of Wilf Carter and Kitty Wells. Many of the poems portray women who drew consolation and strength from those songs of loneliness and heartbreak: and Gregory's rhythms and language often summon up the spirit of Hank Williams.

> His lonesome yodel was really
> Aunty's call disguised
> As a cowboy song,
> Lulling the stars, pulling down
>
> The old Kentucky moon
> So sad and drear
> As she rolled along
> Inside the living room,
>
> Left tears on the kitchen floor,
> Rubbing memories
> From her swollen eyes.
>
> No wonder she took to drinking
> Beer, wine—anything
> For a moment's peace,
> Any reason
> To sit and sing
> How the starts made her blue,
> How tired she was
>
> Scrubbing heaven's floor
> Or holding up the thankless sky
> Right from the snow-covered prairie
> To the blue Canadian Rockies ... [10]

The lives evoked in these poems are often tough, lonely, and tinged with tragedy. Underlying them is a sense of strength, of endurance – the legacy of the two most important women in Gregory's heart.

Writing had always been Gregory's way to understand and come to terms with the events of his life. In his mid-30s, he decided to put his memories on paper. In **Thunder Through My Veins**, Gregory reclaims ownership of his own story.

"There were times that I just wanted to abandon the whole idea...I didn't want to relive any of that stuff...and also, I didn't know how I would feel about strangers reading my story. But it was very therapeutic, being able to see the whole story in its entirety, and being able to take a look back at it."[11]

Some wondered why so young a man was writing a biography. But Gregory didn't want to wait.

"I wanted a freshness to the material. I wanted to be able to talk about my childhood and adolescent experiences with a fresh mind. I didn't want to be writing my life story when I was 50 or 60. I wanted the intensity of the experiences to really shine through."[12]

The book was more for Gregory than an artistic work and a source of healing. It was a lifeline from a survivor, thrown out to other struggling young people.

> **"I didn't want to be writing my life story when I was 50 or 60. I wanted the intensity of the experiences to really shine through."**

"I was hoping to connect with a certain audience, to reach younger people. I knew that there's a lot of value to the book, stuff about poverty, finding your gifts, coming to terms with issues of identity and sexuality. I really wanted to share that process with younger people."

Since writing **Thunder Through My Veins**, Gregory has been re-evaluating his own life and the direction of his writing. He continues to explore his Métis heritage, this time with his Scottish roots and is currently working on a new book of poetry that explores this connection.

"I've been able to acknowledge who I am as an Indigenous person in this country. But I'm also an immigrant here. Those two realities have orchestrated and created the culture that I come out of, the art that I come out of, the dance that I come out of; the stories. Those stories are unique stories. I'm writing about my great, great, great grandparents; and I find that their stories are so powerful and so connected to my own life experiences."

Gregory Scofield is a gay, Métis man. But he has never allowed himself to be defined or limited by those terms. In the end he is a poet and storyteller who, with a stunning command of voice and an extraordinary stylistic range, explores the universal themes of love, acceptance and identity.

Where do I belong, way up north?
The first white trader
Must have felt this way
     on the reserve   a curio looked over
     my skin defies either race   I am neither Scottish or
Cree

So why those disgusted stares?
I speak the language
Eat my bannock with lard

     I am not without history Halfbreed labour built
     this country defending my blood has become a
     life-long occupation

White people have their own ideas
How a real Indian should look
In the city or on the screen

     I've already worked past that   came back to
     the circle my way is not the Indian way or the
     white way

I move in-between

Careful not to shame either side."[13]

NOTES

Excerpts from Gregory Scofield's books appear with permission of the following publishers:

Thunder Through My Veins-HarperFlamingoCanada
Native Canadiana, I Knew Two Metis Women, Love Medicine and One Song—Polestar

[1] Gregory Scofield, *Thunder Through My Veins* (Toronto: Harper Flamingo Canada, 1999) xv.

[2] Linda Richards, "Interview with Gregory Scofield," January magazine. September 1999. http://www.januarymagazine.com/profiles/scofield.html

[3] Gregory Scofield, *Thunder Through My Veins*, 41-42.

[4] Gregory Scofield, *Thunder Through My Veins*, 11.

[5] Linda Richards.

[6] Gregory Scofield, "Piss 'n' Groan," *Native Canadiana*, (Vancouver: Polestar, 1996) 118-119.

[7] Gregory Scofield, "Mixed Breed Act," *Native Canadiana* 56-58.

[8] Gregory Scofield, "Ceremonies," *Love Medicine and One Song* (Vancouver: Polestar, 1997) 91-92.

[9] Gregory Scofield, "Heart Food," *I Knew Two Metis Women* (Vancouver: Polestar, 1999) 16.

[10] Gregory Scofield, "Blue Moon," *I Knew Two Metis Women*, 45-46.

[11] Linda Richards.

[12] John Sinopoli, "Thunder Through His Veins," *WordCulture*, July 24, 2001. www.varsity.utoronto.ca/archives/120/jan24/review/thunder.html

[13] Gregory Scofield, "Between Sides," *The Gathering: Stones from the Medicine Wheel*, (Vancouver: Polestar, 1993) 81.

Major Works by Gregory Scofield

I Knew Two Metis Women. Vancouver: Polestar, 1999.
Love Medicine and One Song. Vancouver: Polestar, 1997.
Native Canadiana: Songs from the Urban Rez. Vancouver: Polestar, 1996.
The Gathering: Stones for the Medicine Wheel. Vancouver: Polestar, 1993.
Thunder Through My Veins. Toronto: HarperFlamingoCanada, 1999.

photo by Columpa C Bobb

Lee Maracle

"I think I was a storyteller when I was born, somehow. I don't have an explanation - but I've always been a storyteller. So I've become moved myself to write the stories that I like to tell." [1]

And there are many stories Lee Maracle likes to tell.

A prolific writer, mother, grandmother, philosopher and activist, Lee first broke new literary ground in autobiographical fiction with **Bobbi Lee: Indian Rebel,** in 1975; decades later, she challenged conventional perspectives on sociology and feminism in *I Am Woman.* The extraordinary range of her work over the years is linked by her rigorous intellect, her unsparing honesty, and her willingness to write as an Aboriginal woman from a place of reality and vulnerability.

A member of the Sto:lo nation, born of a Métis mother, Lee grew up in North Vancouver in a busy household with brothers, sisters, half brothers and sisters, and adopted siblings. Her mother worked during the day, and Lee spent much of her childhood in the company of her grandparents, one of whom was actor and poet Chief Dan George. From her grandparents she first began to learn traditional ways and knowledge.

"I was trained in their language. [The old people] did this for me because they wanted to be able to have a writer that could express themselves", says

Lee. It was their example that inspired her to become a writer.

"The way I spoke was different. All of the people spoke English as poetry. I think that Dan George exemplifies that—those kinds of speakers. They can say poetry at the drop of a hat. That changes how I perceive things, and what I think."

Lee remembers hearing many stories in her family. Not all were easy to understand, and some she has still not unraveled to this day. But she knew from a very young age that storytelling was her gift and her calling.

"I read E. Pauline Johnson when I was nine, and I decided that that was what I wanted to do, because the story changed when she told it." Lee actually tried to resist her vocation as a teenager – but the call was too strong.

> I read E. Pauline Johnson when I was nine, and I decided that that was what I wanted to do, because the story changed when she told it.

She considers herself a mythmaker as opposed to a storyteller. "Storytellers are there to tell the story. But mythmakers are responsible for making that story relevant in the context that we live in. I mull around our old metaphors, our old stories, and try to give them meaning in a modern context, with which to be reborn."

Lee's first major work, **Bobbi Lee: Indian Rebel**, was a fusion of personal experience, traditional storytelling, and social context. Lee came of age in the late 1960s and early 1970s, a time of global upheaval and social change. The Aboriginal world was experiencing the beginnings of the "Red Power" movement, and a new wave of political activism was in the air. Lee's semi-autobiographical account of those turbulent years follows the protagonist, Bobbi Lee, through childhood to maturity.

Bobbi's first encounters with racism come early in life. After meeting the mother of a friend, she recalls her confusion and bewilderment after being told she was not welcome in their house.

> "[My friend] just started crying. Guess she never knew
> that her folks were like that. You know, like when you're
> eleven and watch TV stuff about cowboys and Indians,
> you just don't associate that racist crap with your own
> existence or with your parents' attitudes; it's just exciting
> and something to do after dinner." [2]

This incident is the first in a lifetime of encounters with prejudice and injustice in its many forms - paternalism, sexism, racism, and discrimination. The language is tough and the narrative is unflinching in describing the realities of a life of oppression. Bobbi Lee struggles with apathy, rage, and exhaustion. But she never loses her sense of identity as an Aboriginal woman. And over the course of the book, Bobbi discovers some of the lessons Lee Maracle has learned – the joy of writing, the limits of political solutions, and the capacity of stories to heal, whether within a life or within a culture.

"Poetry and the comfort of my diaries, where truth rolled out of my inner self, began to re-shape me…I became a woman through my words."[3]

Lee understands the power and sacredness of words. To her, words "represent the accumulated knowledge, the progression of thought of any people"[4]. Her novels, poetry and essays are all meant to inspire Aboriginal people to challenge the assumptions and negative stereotypes that define and limit them – sometimes even in their own eyes. Nowhere is her commitment to empowerment clearer than in her 1996 publication, *I Am Woman.*

> *"I mull around our old metaphors, our old stories, and try to give them meaning in a modern context with which to be born."*

I Am Woman is Lee's manifesto, a passionate cry for justice. It is a powerful summary of her vision, as an Aboriginal woman, of life around and inside her, written for Aboriginal people "who need to recover the broken threads of their lives." Building on her memories of childhood, education, social activism and motherhood, Lee links the events of her own life with a broader historical and cultural context, exploring the racism, sexism and colonialism, past and present, that shape Indigenous reality today. Both personal and scholarly, *I Am Woman* is a persuasive and moving analysis of the political and cultural factors defining the feminist and indigenous struggle for equality.

Lee believes that understanding and reclaiming the context of Aboriginal history and identity is an essential part of that struggle. Aboriginal women seek to re-build and re-create the past; but their quest is made more difficult by an "absence of context" and a state of "uncertainty created by the beliefs about ourselves which we inherited and internalized."

"We did not create this history, we had no say in any of the conditions into which we were born, yet we are saddled with the responsibility for altering these conditions and re-building our nations."[5]

> I know nothing
> Of great mysteries
> Know less of creation
> I do know that the farther backward
> In time that I travel
> The more grandmothers
> And the farther forward
> The more grandchildren
> I am obligated to both.[6]

Despite the injustices it describes, Lee sees *I Am Woman* as an optimistic book, and as a tribute, in part, to the resilience and beauty of Aboriginal culture. "I was in such an optimistic state when I wrote that," she says. "I decided at that time that I was going to change the world and the world was going to change....it comes at colonialism from a hundred different levels. And that is the basis for optimism."

Lee's optimism and inspiration has always been the strength of the women in her life, and, in particular, her grandmother. It was her grandmother who encouraged Lee to learn English and understand the ways of Europeans. Internalizing a foreign language and culture was difficult, but her grandmother bluntly pointed out the stark truth of life in a colonized country:

> Master their language daughter; hidden within it is the
> way we are to live among them. It is clear that they will
> never go away. Every year more of them come. England,
> France, Wales—all must be terrible places, for they keep
> coming here to get away from there. I do not begrudge
> them a place here, but why do they have to bequeath to us
> the very things they escape from?"[7]

Sojourners Truth and Other Stories is a collection of stories that Lee describes as "woman-centred" but their scope and impact is universal. These are stories of ordinary people: Aboriginal and non-Aboriginal, young and old, male and female, living on the margins of society. Many of the characters can be seen as tragic: a small boy abused at residential school, an alcoholic, a mother with a deadbeat husband, stretched beyond her limits. But Lee brings them fully, vibrantly to life, and endows with them depth and humanity - as sad as that may be. Full of wit, often painfully personal, her stories are models of spare, effective narrative.

In **Bertha**, the title character is a poor alcoholic living in a slum called Cannery Row. Drunk, exhausted and heartsick, she sits and drinks with a young woman who is getting too old, too quickly. Bertha realizes that young woman has lost her history, her culture and her identity as an Aboriginal woman – and Bertha cannot help her regain them.

> "The brutal realization that she, Bertha, once destined to
> have been this young woman's teacher, had nothing to give
> but stories—dim, only half-remembered and barely
> understood—brought her up short...Bertha wanted to tell
> her about her own unspoiled youth, her hills, the berries,
> the old women, the stories and a host of things she could
> not find the words for in the English she had inherited. It
> was all so paralyzing and mean. Instead Bertha whispered
> her sorrow in the gentle words of their ancestors. They
> were foreign to the girl. The touch, the words, inspired
> only fear in her."[8]

What small comfort Bertha could have offered is denied by the barrier of language: there can be no solace in her culture for the young woman. It is a powerful and moving moment, a painful evocation of the solitude and isolation that comes of separation from culture.

The novel, **Sundogs,** takes place in the summer of 1990. It was the summer of Oka, of Meech Lake, of Elijah Harper. Marianne, a self-described "urban Indian" is adrift. There is no sense of direction in her job, in her love life, in her future. Nothing matters. Emotionally separated from her family, Marianne doesn't fit in – anywhere.

"At home I am not Indian enough and at school, I am much too Indian. The tension wire inside is stretched thin. A few more words and it will snap."[9]

But like most Aboriginal people in Canada, Marianne is shaken by the Oka crisis and by Harper's defeat of the Meech Lake accord: and through the events of 1990, she discovers that some things do matter. She is inspired to learn more about herself and what is important to her.

> *"I thought [Oka] was the most powerful victory that we have ever won. We were worthy of that. It was a moment of recognition that we were not destroyed."*

To Lee, the summer of 1990 was "our day of awakening", a pivotal moment in contemporary Aboriginal history. "It was so rich. I felt that summer that Native people learned about each other," she says. "So much desire to deal with the violence and our environment came out of it. I thought [Oka] was the most powerful victory that we have ever done. We were worthy of that. It was a moment of recognition that we were not destroyed, that you cannot destroy culture, you cannot destroy the spirit of people. You cannot destroy our need to be ourselves."[10]

Historical events also provided the inspiration for Lee's 1993 novel, **Ravensong**, set in the Pacific Northwest coast in the early 1950s. In a community devastated by a flu epidemic, Stacey, the lead character, is finishing her final year of high school and looking toward her future. Like any young woman of the period, she feels pulled in different directions – attracted by the prospect of university and the city, drawn to white culture and its apparent prosperity, repelled by the disease and death overtaking her village. The conflict in her heart is mirrored in the tension between traditionalists in the community and those who want to embrace change and mainstream society.

As the story unfolds, Stacey becomes increasingly conscious of the apathy of the "white" townsfolk, who seem indifferent to the ravages of the flu among her people. She faces the growing realization that she is marginal – an "other". She decides to attend university, and then reconsiders her decision.

> "She wonders about her obsession with going to their university and her family's faith in the sanity of her obsession. "How else are we to learn how we are to live with them?" Dominic had said. Both Old Nora and Ella had agreed. Was that it? She wondered. Is the whole point of her going to UBC to learn how to live with them? She was tired. Looking is so hard." [11]

Woven through the novel and implied in the title is the presence of Raven –
not the familiar male, West coast trickster figure, but a decidedly female entity,
weeping over the devastating changes in the community and its lack of spiritual
guidance. To Lee, Raven represents that guidance; she is a catalyst for change,
for transformation. "[Raven] doesn't necessarily transform things in a good
way, but Raven is the transformer or the harbinger of transformation in our
culture," says Lee. "Our culture is a culture that looks upon life as constant
spiritual growth and social transformation."[12]

While Raven seeks a mystical awakening and spiritual understanding between
the two cultures, Stacey must establish her own balance between her
community and the world outside. Her challenge is to engage and learn to
live in, and learn from, both. But it is her roots in the community and her
tradition that will anchor her as she moves away from home.

> "White folks, even her friend Carol, all seemed to be so
> rudderless. Because of that the kids at school seemed to
> suffer from a kind of frantic desperation. Maybe no roots
> was the problem. Maybe some white people had no roots
> in the creative process…if you have only yourself as a start
> and end point, life becomes a pretence at continuum."[13]

Lee Maracle's most constant theme - the strength that flows from knowledge
of self and culture – is at the heart of **Daughters are Forever,** the book she
found most difficult to write.

Marilyn is an Aboriginal social worker, alienated from her culture, family
and self. As she works with a young mother who neglected and abused her
baby, Marilyn must come to terms with her own failings as a mother. But
without an understanding of the past or a sense of connection to her culture,
Marilyn is powerless to understand the present, or find reconciliation with
her own estranged daughters.

That knowledge is represented by the character Westwind, the natural world,
and the voice of her tradition.

> "Westwind follows Marilyn. He whispers old story as he
> tugs and nags at her coattails. He is always beside her. He
> pleads with her to listen. But Marilyn has no memories of
> reassurance, no cultivation of thought processes that
> would guide her to hear Westwind…she does not hear the
> Westwind-borne voices of her ancestors whispering in her
> ear."[14]

Built on a unique narrative structure based on Salish storytelling, the novel is
an indictment of the outsiders who took their children away to residential
schools and foster homes, and of Aboriginal men who degraded and dismissed
female wisdom in favour of "white" ways.

The story ends on a note of redemption. By learning once again to hear the voice of the wind, Marilyn begins to heal the lifelong emotional wounds that have severed her from her daughters. It is a healing that Lee had to undergo herself.

"I had to come with reconciliation [to my own family] before I could complete the book. It was difficult. I wanted to capture the concept of inherited hurt because it was something I was going through."

Though Lee has been widely acclaimed by mainstream critics and audiences, she writes primarily for an Aboriginal readership. Early in her career, she did not want to publish; she knew "white people would be reading". But in the end it was the writing that mattered. She simply had to tell the stories.

"I feel that all our people are thinking people. They come from thinking cultures. There's a huge level of awareness that doesn't exist among white folks because white folks can afford to be apathetic. Ours can't."[15]

Lee believes that a key facet of Aboriginal consciousness and awareness is memory, both personal and collective. "We are an oral people: history, law, politics, sociology, the self, and our relationship to the world are all contained in our memory...we are who we are by what we remember and what we do not."[16]

Memory is a theme explored in many of Lee's stories, and a key to her perception of her role as an author. She writes to help all Aboriginal people remember who they are. "A lot of our people say we suffer from low self-esteem, but I don't think that's the case. I think we have a sense of dignity, but no context to talk to ourselves about it...those who went to residential school didn't have the right words so they had nothing to fight with. Until we find those words, we need encouragement from each other. And then we can take on the world."

We are who we are by what we remember and what we do not.

Lee is working on several new projects. She is seeking to "do more universal-type writings" that have resonance with a wide readership, while continuing to look within her culture and inspiring others to do the same.

She knows there will always be more stories to tell.

> I am moved by my love for human life;
> By the firm conviction that all the world
> Must stop the butchery, stop the slaughter.
> I am moved by my scars, by my own filth
> To re-write history with my body
> To shed the blood of those who betray themselves.
> To life, world humanity I ascribe
> To my people...my history...I address
> My vision.[17]

Notes

Excerpts from Lee Maracle's books appear courtesy of the following publishers:

Bobbi Lee, Indian Rebel—Women's Press, Toronto.
I Am Woman, Sojourners and Sundogs, Ravensong—Press Gang Publishers, Vancouver.
Daughters are Forever—Polestar, Vancouver.
Bent Box—Theytus Books, Penticton.

[1] Jennifer Kelly, "A Conversation with Lee Maracle," Ariel, 25.1 January, 1994. Calgary: University of Calgary. pg. 76.

[2] Lee Maracle, **Bobbi Lee, Indian Rebel.** Toronto: Women's Press, 1990: 49.

[3] **Bobbi Lee,** pg. 230.

[4] **Bobbi Lee**, pg. 7.

[5] Lee Maracle, **I Am Woman**, Vancouver, Press Gang, 1996. x.

[6] Lee Maracle, **I Am Woman**, 8.

[7] Lee Maracle, **I Am Woman**, 65-66.

[8] Lee Maracle, **Sojourners and Sundogs**. Vancouver: Press Gang Publishers, 1999. pg. 231.

[9] Lee Maracle, **Sojourners and Sundogs**. Vancouver: Press Gang Publishers, 1999. pg. 25.

[10] A Conversation with Lee Maracle, pg. 77.

[11] Lee Maracle, **Ravensong**. Vancouver : Press Gang Publishers, 1993. pg. 154.

[12] A Conversation with Lee Maracle, pg. 74.

[13] Lee Maracle, **Ravensong**. Vancouver: Press Gang Publishers, 1993 pg. 61.

[14] Lee Maracle, **Daughters are Forever.** Vancouver: Polestar, 2002. pg. 38-39.

[15] A Conversation with Lee Maracle, pg. 81.

[16] **My Home as I Remember**, edited by Lee Maracle and Sandra Laronde. Toronto: Natural Heritage Books, 2000. pg. i.

[17] "War" Lee Maracle, **Bent Box**. Penticton, BC: Theytus Books, 2000. pg. 51.

Major Works by Lee Maracle

Bent Box. Penticton: Theytus Books, 2000

Bobbi Lee, Indian Rebel. Toronto: Women's Press, 1990.

Daughters are Forever. Vancouver: Polestar, 2002.

I Am Woman. Vancouver: Press Gang Publishers, 1996.

Ravensong. Vancouver : Press Gang Publishers, 1993

Sojourners and Sundogs. Vancouver: Press Gang Publishers, 1999.

Will's Garden. Penticton: Theytus Books, 2002.

Editor of ***My Home as I Remember***, with Sandra Laronde. Toronto: Natural Heritage Books, 2000.

Other stories in various anthologies, essays in magazines.

Louise Halfe

"Old one with laughing eyes
Wrap me in blanket grass
Fragrant with sweet pine,
The woman-musk
Of your rain fed forest.
Ground my wandering feet."[1]

Many times during her life, Louise Halfe pulled up stakes, moved from her home reserve of Saddle Lake, Alberta, and let her wandering feet carry her across Canada. Sometimes the journey was her own idea, and sometimes it was not. But throughout her travels, Louise has remained grounded in her Cree culture, in her identity as a woman in a family of strong women, and in her work as a writer.

Louise's first trip off the reserve happened before she was born, perhaps the sign of a wandering life to come.

"I was born in the middle of a Ukrainian town called Two-Hills Alberta. That's at least 20 miles from the reserve. My mother travelled there on the back of a tractor while she was in labour. There we were, bouncing along, riding that tractor to town!"

Louise's description of her early home life sounds idyllic and traditional. "Off the gravel road there was a log cabin. It's now burned down, but that's where most of my memories are…my grandmother had her own sweatlodge, and my grandfather was her helper. I was a watcher and I watched my grandmother, especially when she would make her medicines."

But the reality of her early life was not so peaceful. Alcohol had a powerful and devastating influence on her family. "Those times weren't happy times. There was family violence. I was traumatized that way."

Those early, conflicting memories of pain and tranquility would become a wellspring of material for Louise's early poetry.

I'm going to take you home, Mama
Yes, to that log shack where Papa skilled beaver on the dirt floor.
The grass is tall. There'll be lots of mosquitoes.
Yes, Mama, the old fridge is still there and no, there's no
Lightning going through it make it breathe.
The windows are broken and the barn swallows have built
Their nest where the stovepipe used to smoke.
Oh Mama don't, Papa hasn't walked on that land, not for
Years. Not since the last time he crushed your ribs on that
Fridge.
He's on skid row somewhere.
It's safe. All we have are the old ghosts, drifting
Through the clouds of our heads.
…
Yes, we're almost there.
I can see the old shack, the outhouse, the chicken coop,
The jalopy.
Yes, Mama we're going home. No more hiding.[2]

Louise's grandmother had a profound effect on her life, providing a spiritual foundation when she was a young child. From her grandmother Louise learned the traditional ways of the Cree people, including their ceremonies and medicine. Loving memories of her grandmother frequently emerge in her poetry.

The brown labouring bear
Nôhkom, the medicine woman
Alone in her attic den
Smoking slim cigarettes
Wears the perfume of sage, sweetgrass
And earth medicine ties.
Nôhkom, the medicine bear
Healer of troubled spirits.
A red kerchief on her head.
Blonde-white braids hang down below her breasts.

> She hums her medicine songs
> Shuffling alone in her den where
> No light penetrates, no secrets escape...[3]

"For me, life was a mixture of blessings and curses at home because I grew up with alcoholism and family violence - but at the same time, with the contradiction of living a very traditional lifestyle. That's still very much a part of me; it's like I still wear the skins of the old people."

When she was six years old, Louise was sent to the Blue Quills residential school in St. Paul, more than 20 miles from the reserve.

"Such shame. Such assault. That's what it was, refined under the rule of reading, writing and arithmetic, and a god that had the eyes of a roving fly. This god wore black robes, cowls, and beads."[4] Though she rarely talks about her experiences there, Louise believes that residential school had a profound and lifelong impact on any child who attended – for better, or for worse. Some children grew into rebels, rejecting structure, discipline and everything else they learned in school; others stopped resisting, and surrendered to the system's rigid demands. But no-one escaped unchanged; and the experience left many marks.

> A yellow caterpillar,
> It swallows them up.
> The little brown ones their stained
> Faces in the windows   skinny and thick
> Black braids   pressing hands
> Grease the glass...
> The building is huge
> With long white empty hallways.
> A child walks softly
> The echo runs ahead of her.
> The smell of Lysol
> And floor wax
> Overwhelms the memory of wood smoke
> And dirt floors.[5]

Between the ages of six and fourteen, Louise was shuttled between residential school and public schools in nearby St. Paul. During the summer, she traveled with her family to southern Alberta, where they worked in the sugar beet fields.

Louise spent her high school years moving from school to school across Alberta, struggling to fit in and to survive.

"I always thought of quitting school because I had poor self-esteem. I focussed on trying to be a secretary because I didn't have any high aspirations; I wasn't encouraged. "

It was during those difficult teen years that Louise discovered the gift that would change her life – her writing. Ironically, she first found her path by losing a contest.

In grade nine, Louise entered a writing competition sponsored by a local radio station. Her entry was an essay about the conflict in Vietnam, a country and a war she now cheerfully acknowledges she knew virtually nothing about. She did not win the contest: but she did win the consolation prize - a book called "I Am an Indian." It wasn't particularly well written, Louise recalls; but was her first taste of Native writing and she "took pleasure in it."[6]

That book, acquired by chance, led her to begin her own writing journey.

"I started writing when I was a teenager because I was suicidal. I turned to writing to try to find expression. That's not to say that writing is a form of therapy or healing, because I don't believe that. I think it's like a catharsis; it sort of shows you where to go, but you do your own healing - not the writing."

> **"I started writing when I was a teenager because I was suicidal. I turned to writing to try to find expression.**

Like many writers, Louise began jotting down her thoughts and putting them into journals. The act of formalizing her ideas and writing them out was an important catalyst that sparked her imagination. But those journals, her first creative writing, were intensely personal, and Louise later destroyed many of them.

"It's a cleansing ritual, burning some of those journals. Every five years I burn them and keep some things that I think I can use for future reference. I don't want to hurt anybody because of my writing. A lot of what I write is my own private garbage and ranting."

All through her teenage years and into her twenties, when she married and began to raise her two children, Louise continued to write for herself. It was only after her children entered school that she began to consider her writing more seriously.

"In the process of keeping a journal, poetry took form. I never fought it. I completely trusted it. My dreams forecasted my journey long before I understood that I was to be a writer.[7] I think most people are chosen by poetry. Poetry can say so much in so few words. I tried to be a playwright once, but I struggled so much with it, and I realized I was wasting my time. You do what the spirit tells you."

And that spirit told Louise to keep writing poetry. In 1994, drawing together the best work from her years of journals, Louise published her first book of poetry, **Bear Bones and Feathers.**

The motif of bones was an appropriate metaphor for Louise's life; it was an image rich in connotation. "Writing, for me, can be a process of baring myself— to lick, tear, strip stories from my bones."[8] Bones are an important element in making medicine; to Louise, stories are medicine as well. "The whole earth is made of bones and ashes. Why are we so fascinated with bones? Because we are filled with the spirit of bone, that's why. That spirit is the Creator—the bone of the Creator."

"The prairie is full of bones. The bones stand and sing and I feel the weight of them as they guide my fingers on this page."[9]

> I think most people are chosen by poetry. Poetry can say so much in so few words. I tried to be a playwright once but I realized I was wasting my time. You do what the spirit tells you.

Bear Bones and Feathers is a cycle of autobiographical poems of loss, family, and tradition. Louise interweaves stories of reserve life with residential school experiences and the surprising vagaries of love. In several poems, she writes in dialect, evoking the voice of her Cree ancestors as they spoke English. In a series of humorous letters written to the Pope, Louise uses that distinctive voice to point out injustice.

> I wonder if you could dell da govment
> To make dem laws dat stop dat
> Whiteman from dakin our isistâwina (rituals)
> Cuz i dell you pope
> I don't dink you like it
> If i dook you
> Gold cup and wine
> Pass it 'round our circles
> Cuz i don't have you drainin
> From doze schools.
> I haven't married you jeesuz
> And i don't kneel to him,
> Cuz he ain't my god.[10]

"That thick toned speech with an accent, that's beautiful. There's nothing to be ashamed of when you speak because it's got its own beauty and if that's the way you choose to write in a creative way then write with it." Louise believes that writing in this style gives people "…permission to say: I am not ashamed." It is a way for Aboriginal writers to challenge the literary establishment and give a true, resonant voice to perspectives that are too seldom heard.

Bear Bones and Feathers was a critical success. It won the 1996 Milton Acorn People's Poetry Award, and was nominated for both the Spirit of Saskatchewan Award and the Pat Lowther First Book Award.

Louise's second book of poetry, **Blue Marrow,** was published in 1998 and nominated for a Governor General's Award for poetry. It was inspired by a discussion with an elder about the telling of history.

"After I finished **Bear Bones and Feathers**, he asked me what I was going to do. At that point I didn't have a clue. I said, "Well, I've been thinking for a long time now that I really should rewrite history." We just laughed because it's a ludicrous idea, really, a really wild idea. And he said, "Why not? And I said, "You're right, why not?"[11]

Blue Marrow intertwines historical stories of Aboriginal women with those of the white men they married. She writes from their differing perspectives, a technique that creates a jarring counterpoint of personal and historical responses.

> "That thick toned speech with an accent, that's beautiful. There's nothing to be ashamed of when you speak because it's got its own beauty."

"The little ones with dirty blond hair
look at me with dawn's eyes. I travel with them
into their backyard
where those men of god docked their ships,
took brown wives,
left them in barns and stalls—
horseflies and mosquitos"."[12]

The strong undercurrent of anger in these poems echoes the emotion aroused by Louise's examination of archival records of European settlers in Canada. The newcomers tried to write with compassion; but their arrogance, self-righteousness and racism were unmistakable. "And I was grateful for that because it allowed the voices in **Blue Marrow** to speak directly from that onslaught. It allowed me to go to my very bone to respond with healthy anger and deep pain."[13]

"It was not the only time
I hated the man
Whose white flesh
Shared my bed.
My memory
Snared by my people, beggars in the land
That once filled their bellies.
I still see those
Grandmothers clench the Bundles,
Whisper songs through the night."[14]

Canadian history is full of mixed marriages, but little has been written about how Aboriginal women felt about their situations, why they married Europeans, or what their lives were like. **Blue Marrow** is a poet's creative answer to those questions. The book's Aboriginal women often choose and desire these white, foreign men, but suffer disillusionment when they are abandoned or replaced by white women arriving from Europe.

"I wasn't dead when he took his white bride.
Didn't I tell you all along I've been a breeding
Horse galloping? Fed to dogs,
I rotted.
How many times as I lay beneath him did he remind me
I am the bargain from my father's trade?

How many times did he raise my dress,
Sweated hands smeared with dirt and cow,
Bloody from skinning? And I received him joyfully.
I am a gentleman's wife."[15]

Much of the inspiration for Louise's writing comes from dreams and visions. "That's where a lot of my writing comes from. It's not only my dream place; but there's my daydreaming, or what some call fantasy. That's where my images come from, where my material comes from."

Mixed ancestry is a recurring thread throughout Louise's poetry. It is a theme many Aboriginal people struggle with, and one with deep personal significance for Louise.

"My ancestry is Cree and probably French. My kids are Norwegian, British, Cree and French. It was hard for me to say I am not full-blood, but I think that's why I like writing - because you do call on the conqueror and the conquered. I think [mixed blood people] have this flexibility, this ability to stretch and to gather and expand in a way that the person who is only of one blood cannot. So you have a whole facet of places that you can pour into; this wonderful blessing of cascading water into your being that makes you the person that you are, and gives you the ability to see things one way rather than another."

Louise Halfe draws her poetry from the many facets of her personality, and reaches for inspiration deep within her life experience. Some readers have told her that her writing can seem angry and bitter. But Louise remains true to the voices that inspire her to write; she's not afraid to speak about issues that others prefer to keep hidden.

"I don't dictate what I should write and what I shouldn't write. I have to be true to whatever is guiding me. And if I'm dark and angry, so be it. Anger can be used in a powerful way to bring a person out of a helpless state and into action...I want to believe my anger is constructive - that my anger sees with the eyes of our Trickster and shows the story."[16]

> "I think [mixed blood people] have this flexibility, this ability to stretch and to gather and expand in a way that the person who is only of one blood cannot."

At its deepest level, the poetry of Louise Halfe reflects a profound affirmation and love of life. Her goal is not to dictate a single perspective or vision; she hopes her work will help readers to find their own truths.

"Stories bring readers to self-discovery and whatever it is they discover, it is for themselves, and if they choose to share, I, too, become the student. Writing, if done well, lifts the veils of our own pain, our own ignorance."[17]

NOTES ————————————————————————————————

Excerpts from Louise Halfe's books have been quoted with permission of Coteau Books.

[1] Louise Halfe, "Nohkom atayohkan 1", **Bear Bones and Feathers**. (Regina, Sask: Coteau Books, 1994) 10.

[2] Louise Halfe, "Fog Inside Mama," **Bear Bones and Feathers** 44-45.

[3] Louise Halfe, "Nôhkom, Medicine Bear", **Bear Bones and Feathers** 13-14.

[4] "Returning," **Bear Bones and Feathers** 105.

[5] "The Residential School Bus," **Bear Bones and Feathers** 65.

[6] Esta Spalding, "Interview with Louise Halfe," **Brick magazine** # 60, Fall, 1998: 44.

[7] Spalding 43.

[8] Jeannette Armstrong & Lally Grauer, ed, "Louise Halfe" **Native Poetry in Canada; a Contemporary Anthology**. (Penticton: Theytus Books, 2001) 240.

[9] Louise Halfe, "Introduction", **Blue Marrow.** (Regina, Sask: Coteau Books, 1998)

[10] Louise Halfe, "My Ledders," **Bear Bones and Feathers** 103.

[11] Spalding, 44.

[12] Halfe, **Blue Marrow** 11.

[13] Spalding 45.

[14] Halfe, **Blue Marrow** 30.

[15] Halfe, **Blue Marrow** 52.

[16] "Interview with Louise Halfe," p. 47.

[17] "Louise Halfe," **Native Poetry in Canada; a Contemporary Anthology,** p. 239.

Major Works by Louis Halfe

Bear Bones and Feathers. Regina: Coteau Books, 1994.

Blue Marrow. Regina: Coteau Books, 1998.

Basil Johnston

Basil Johnston's prolific writing career - more than a dozen books, countless articles and essays - began with a single, innocuous question from a 10-year-old boy.

It was during the late 1960s. A grade five class was studying Indians, and Basil was reviewing their elaborate displays.

"There was this one sour-looking guy in front of his tipi. I greeted him. "How!" He said he had always wanted to be an Indian, and he thought he would learn something. But he said he hadn't learned anything."

Then came the question.

"He said, "Is that all there is to Indians?""

That plaintive, perceptive query got Basil thinking. He began to investigate the books about Aboriginal people then available to students and teachers, and reached the same disappointing conclusion. No wonder his interrogator from grade five was bored with the topic of Indians; Basil found nothing but texts stuffed with dry facts about hunting, gathering and social practices – no hint of the richness, complexity, humour and joy of Aboriginal culture.

Just a few months later, Basil was warming up for a presentation to an Aboriginal educational conference. When he asked the participants what aspect of Aboriginal culture they particularly wanted him to discuss, a member of the group growled, "Just tell us about your heritage."

"The tone and the gist of that demand set me back so that I stammered and stumbled. I guess I survived, but it made me think about these things. That's when I decided I wanted to write."

That was back in the late 1960s. Over the last three decades, Basil Johnston has done an extraordinary job of meeting the need for books that capture the essence of Aboriginal life. His many works on heritage, culture and language have introduced an international readership to the world of Ojibway storytelling, humour and spirituality; and his willingness to explore his own life and memories have brought forth deeply personal books about residential schools, families, communities, and disability.

> *Basil was a curious boy, a keen observer with a sharp memory; and his life soon provided him with ample material for his own stories.*

Born on the Parry Island reserve in central Ontario, Basil grew up in Cape Croker, immersed in the Ojibway language and the stories of his community. As a child, he formed strong relationships with many local elders, and his early contact with their stories and knowledge provided a rich background for his later writing on Ojibway history, legends and cultural practices. But Basil was a curious boy, a keen observer with a sharp memory; and his life soon provided him with ample material for his own stories. Sent to residential school at the age of ten, he experienced the events that eventually formed the basis of his first autobiographical work - **Indian School Days**, an engaging and highly personal memoir of his life at St. Peter Claver's school in Spanish, near Sudbury in northern Ontario.

In his introduction to **Indian School Days**, Basil reflects on the brutality of a government that systematically took children from their homes and on the devastating effects this policy had on individuals, families and communities.

"The mothers and grandmothers cried and wept, as mine did, in helplessness and heartache. There was nothing, absolutely nothing that they could do, as women and as Indians, to reverse the decision of 'the Department.' Already many had suffered the anguish of separation from husbands, now they had to suffer further the anguish of being dispossessed of their children; later, they would have to endure alienation from the children who were sent away to Spanish."[1]

But **Indian School Days** is not overtly political; nor is it angry or bitter. It is a book of highly personal stories, told from the vantage point of a young boy with a very keen eye. Priests, parents and playmates emerge as real, memorable, finely-etched characters, described with clarity and compassion. The author faithfully captures the rhythms and moods of day-to-day life at the school, from the monotony of dormitory routine to the covert excitement of schoolboy insurrection, from the tedium of institutional food to the magic of summer holidays.

The tone is warm, affectionate, and – surprisingly - very funny. Many Aboriginal people suffered terrible abuse at residential schools, and have only traumatic memories of their experiences. But laughter has always been an important part of healing, and Basil says he prefers to dwell on the humorous side of school, and of life.

"(I was told), 'these stories are funny, why don't you write them down?' So I wrote them down, and eventually they made up the text. Of course there's a dark side...but I want to leave that behind. You have to go on with your life. You can't wallow in self-pity."

> Of course there's a dark side...but I want to leave that behind. You have to go on with your life. You can't wallow in self-pity.

It is humour, as much as compassion that transforms **Indian School Days** from a "residential school book" to something more timeless and broader in its appeal.

After eight years in residential school, Basil tried his hand at a number of traditional jobs: hunting, trapping, farming, and a stint in the lumber industry. But none of these seemed like the trade for him. After studying law in university, he also decided against a legal career. He liked the idea of a two-month holiday every summer, though; so Basil entered teachers college, and graduated in 1962.

In the late 1960s, Basil was invited to by Dr. E.S. Rogers to assist the Royal Ontario Museum in developing Aboriginal history courses and curriculum materials. Given the incentive and opportunity to write down many of the traditional stories he remembered from childhood, he produced **Ojibway Heritage**. Published in 1976, it is a vibrant evocation of his people's life, legends, and beliefs.

In his preface, Basil suggests that to understand Aboriginal heritage, one must examine ceremonies, rituals, songs, dances, prayers, and stories. These illustrate the "sum total of what people believe about life, being, existence...It is in story, fable, legend, and myth that fundamental understandings, insights, and attitudes toward life and human conduction, character and quality in their diverse forms are embodied and passed on."[2]

The book interweaves stories about the creation of the world and the nature of plants and animals with vivid and accurate descriptions of ceremonies, songs and dances. One of its most intriguing sections introduces readers to the Midewewin, a sacred Ojibway medicine society.

"In the beginning, admission to the Midewewin required only knowledge of plants and the power of healing. With the introduction of morality into medicine practice, members were required to possess good characters...admission into the Midewewin was by invitation only."[3]

Some authors are uncomfortable dealing with matters of spirit and ceremony, feeling, perhaps, that such knowledge should not be shared outside the culture.

But Basil believes these truths must be recorded - as long as the writer is knowledgeable.

"I know what I'm writing about. I think there is a need to write this down. The word 'spiritual' in English is always connected with 'religious.' For me the spiritual is right there. There is nothing mystical about spirituality. It's everyday life—you can see it, you can hear it, you can feel it. That's spirituality."

Ojibway Heritage was the first of several books Basil has written about Ojibway ceremonies and stories. He continued to write about Ojibway spirituality in **The Manitous: The Spiritual World of the Ojibway.** It is a topic that fascinates him.

"Stories about the manitous allow native people to understand their cultural and spiritual heritage, and enable them to see the worth and relevance of their ideas, institutions, perceptions, and values. Once they see the worth and relevance of their heritage, they may be inspired to restore it in their lives."[4]

Basil's writings on Ojibway spirituality reveal both his own enthusiasm for the subject and his passion for encouraging Aboriginal people to retain their language and culture. As a teacher, writer and storyteller, he believes that language is the key to cultural survival. If Aboriginal languages are lost, then Aboriginal peoples' understanding of their own heritage will be lost as well; language is the vehicle through which the cultural legacy is conveyed to future generations. "No longer will they think Indian or feel Indian...they will have lost their identity which no amount of reading can ever restore. Only language and literature can restore the "Indianness."[5] Basil has always encouraged and assisted scholars who wish to learn about Ojibway culture; but he insists they must study the language if they want to truly understand the people.

> *"I know what I'm writing about. I think there is a need to write this down. The word 'spiritual' in English is always connected with 'religious.' For me, the spiritual is right there. There's northing mystical about it."*

As part of his commitment to the language, Basil has written several course manuals and hopes to develop an Ojibway thesaurus.. He wants to encourage language teachers to go beyond simple grammar and linguistics instruction, and infuse their lessons with a true sense of the culture. "What can be so interesting when we're just doing grammar and linguistics? Language teachers aren't trained in history or literature so they could blend these disciplines."

Apart from his autobiographical and educational work, Basil may be best known as a writer of humour and satire in such collections as **Moose Meat and Wild Rice.** Published in 1978, these stories explore the lives of the inhabitants of the fictional Moose Meat Point Indian reserve, near the town of Blunder Bay. His characters are both realistic and caricatures, occasionally verging on the stereotypical - the welfare bum, the alcoholic, and the lazy worker. But for Basil, honesty and humour are more important than political correctness. He feels that people sometimes take themselves too seriously; as an antidote, he takes delight in poking fun at everyone. "People worry too much about stereotypes. If you're going to be a stereotype, you might as well be the best damn stereotype there is. These people are funny!"

He sets out his satirist's manifesto in the preface: "I dedicate this book to storytellers, listeners, and to all good Moose Meat people; to those with a sense of humour; I dedicate this book especially to the white man, without whose customs and evangelistic spirit the events recounted would not have occurred."[6]

> *He feels that people sometimes take themselves too seriously; as an antidote, he takes delight in poking fun at everyone.*

Basil claims a special affection for the absurd and improbable, and insists that all the stories in **Moose Meat and Wild Rice** are true. "Stupid things inspire me, dumb things", he says. "You watch, you read, you listen. Lots of dumb things come out of that."

Like the tale of the two canoeists who decided to get a free ride by hitching their canoe to a swimming moose. It might have worked, if only they'd been able to shoot the moose before it charged out of the water and up the hill, leaving the canoeists drenched and sprawled amid the wreckage of their canoes and supplies.

Or old Kitug-Aunquot, who was chastised by the priest for eating bologna on a Friday. "Bologna is meat", said the priest sternly. "It's many different kinds of meat". Kitug-Aunquot got the last word when he was asked to help haul wood for the priest and instead delivered - sawdust.

> "Kitug-Aunquot, what in the name of damnation are you doing?" asked the priest.
>
> "Bring wood, fauder," Kitug-Aunquot answered calmly.
>
> "But this is sawdust. It isn't wood! Are you trying to make a fool of me?" the priest demanded, his hands on his hips.
>
> "Fauder, you say boloney meat. Okay; then sawdus' is woods," Kitug-Aunquot declared with a twinkle in his eye."[7]

Basil's tongue-in-cheek narrative and deadpan accounts of absurd events are reminiscent of Mark Twain or Stephen Leacock; and like those authors, his stories and characters become more universal than their settings.

The scope and diversity of Basil Johnston's work was already impressive when, in 2002, he published his most personal and reflective book to date. **Crazy Dave** is a memoir of Basil's uncle David McLeod, who suffered from Down's syndrome. It was a story he had wanted to write for many years. His uncle had been a strong, stubborn and remarkable man, living a difficult life in an incomprehensible world. **Crazy Dave** is both biography and a profound reflection on community, family, and love.

"I guess I started to write some of the episodes in my uncle's life, offering these humorous incidents or misadventures that he suffered, and they were all unconnected. I had one false start and I realized that something was missing—that I could not leave my grandmother out of it."[8]

The book celebrates Dave's life, but also the family and community where he lived. Particularly moving is the evocation of Rosa McLeod, Basil's grandmother and Dave's mother.

"Uncle David depended on her almost completely. Grandmother looked after him, worried about him, subordinated her life to his so that he could lead his life and existence as well as he could. She, too, needed someone. She needed David - not to the same extent that he needed her, but she needed him. She needed company. She needed someone to care for."[9]

Crazy Dave is at times funny, affectionate, and heartbreaking – sometimes simultaneously. Anecdotes from Dave's life – his premature ringing of the Angelus bell, his father's futile attempts to teach him to fish – underscore the difficulty of living in a community when one is different from everyone else. But they also illuminate Dave's humanity.

As the story of "Crazy Dave's" life unfolds, the reader becomes increasingly aware of the disturbing parallels between Dave's life – a man struggling to survive and adapt to a too-complex world – and the struggle of Aboriginal people to define a place for themselves in the context of modern Canada.

> *This is also a story, albeit sketchy, of a native people attempting to regain a little of what they once had in abundance.*

"This is also a story, albeit sketchy, of a native people attempting to regain a little of what they once had in abundance: freedom, equality, independence, land, pride, justice, dreams, and the chance to show and to say, "This I can do.""[10]

Many people tolerated Crazy Dave, sheltered him, and treated him kindly – as long as he "behaved". But when he failed to act as they felt he should, he was mocked, chastised, and punished. Basil sees in that treatment an echo of those unfortunate Aboriginal people who are forced to "behave" – to abandon their beliefs, their values, and their culture, and adopt the ways of the dominant culture – in order to win acceptance and get ahead.

Ultimately, however, the book is not a political allegory. It's a labour of love, honouring a man who once held an important place in his family – a man still remembered with affection, years after his death.

Crazy Dave is not, strictly speaking, a "memoir". Basil 's only memories of his uncle are drawn from the few years that he lived on the reserve as a child. Most of the book's details and events come from recollections of sisters, uncles, cousins and friends. But Basil feels that scholarly, formal investigation is not always the best path to the truth.

"There's too much emphasis on research," he says. "Research reveals that there is written documentation; but we don't have a lot of written documentation. I distrust diarists. Diarists set down what enhances their works and their reputations; omit what is or may be injurious to them, because they will not admit to commission of dark deeds or errors." In the introduction to **Crazy Dave**, Basil emphasizes the importance of oral history.

"The stories and opinions I have used as sources for this book will not be found in the band council minute book, or in the diaries of the clergy, or in the archives of the *Wiarton Echo* or in the *Owen Sound Sun Times*, but are stored in the memories of the older generation still living."

Those memories – the legacy of a past shared by friends, elders, relatives and community members - have been Basil Johnston's richest source. From his earliest cultural writings to his latest book, **Honour Earth Mother,** published by Kegedonce Press, he has given new form and a new voice to the ancient oral tradition, carrying old truths to a new generation.

"I don't know if any of my books have made a difference although I would like to think that they have, " he says. "I satisfy myself by saying at least I tried."

Notes

Excerpts from Basil Johnston's books appear with permission of the following publishers:

Indian School Days, **Crazy Dave**—Key Porter Books
Moose Meat and Wild Rice—McClelland and Stewart

[1] Basil Johnston, **Indian School Days** (Toronto: Key Porter Books, 1988) 8.

[2] Basil Johnston, **Ojibway Heritage** (New York: Columbia University, 1976) 7.

[3] Basil Johnston, **Ojibway Heritage**, 84.

[4] Basil Johnston, **The Manitous: Spiritual World of the Ojibway** (Toronto: HarperCollins, 1995) xii.

[5] Basil H. Johnston, "One Generation from Extinction," Native Writers and Canadian Writing. **Canadian Literature**, special issue (Vancouver: UBC Press, 1990) 10.

[6] Basil Johnston, **Moose Meat and Wild Rice** (Toronto: McClelland & Stewart, 1978) 9.

[7] Basil Johnston, *Moose Meat and Wild Rice*, 84.

[8] Pat St. Germain, "*Crazy Dave*," Winnipeg Sun 25 Sept. 1999.

[9] Basil Johnston, *Crazy Dave* (Toronto: Key Porter Books, 1999) 13.

[10] Basil Johnston, *Crazy Dave*, 14.

Major Works by Basil Johnston

By Canoe and Moccasins: Some Native Place Names of the Great Lakes. Lakefield: Waapoone Publishing, 1986.

Crazy Dave. Toronto: Key Porter Books, 1999.

Honour Earth Mother. Cape Croker: Kegedonce Press, 2003.

How the Birds Got Their Colours. Toronto: Kids Can Press, 1978.

Indian School Days. Toronto: Key Porter Books, 1988.

Mermaids and Medicine Women. Toronto: Royal Ontario Museum, 1998.

Moose Meat and Wild Rice. Toronto: McClelland & Stewart, 1978.

Ojibway Ceremonies. Toronto: McClelland & Stewart, 1982.

Ojibway Heritage. New York: Columbia University, 1976.

Tales of the Anishinaubae: Ojibway Legends. Toronto: University of Toronto, 1994.

Tales the Elders Told: Ojibway Legends. Toronto: Royal Ontario Museum, 1981.

The Bear-Walker and Other Stories. Toronto: Royal Ontario Museum, 1985.

The Manitous: the Spiritual World of the Ojibway. Toronto: HarperCollins, 1995.

Publications also include articles and essays in various anthologies and periodicals across Canada.

photo by Greg Young-Ing

Jeannette Armstrong

...I am the dreamer
The choice maker
The word speaker
I speak in a language of words
Formed of the actions of the past
Words that become the sharing
The collective knowing
The links that become a people
The dreaming that becomes a history
The calling forth of voices
And sending forward of memory
I am the weaver of memory thread
Twining past to future
I am the artist
The storyteller...[1]

As a poet, novelist and speaker, Jeannette Armstrong has carried the voices and stories of her beloved Okanagan to the world; and by helping to establish Canada's first Aboriginal publishing house and a pre-eminent creative writing program, she has nurtured a whole new generation of indigenous writers.

Jeannette's deepest inspiration as an artist and activist has always been her enduring connection to her community and culture. Unlike many of her generation, she never lost the sense of her own identity.

"My family lives in a remote part of our community, and I feel very fortunate that I grew up with our traditions, our language, our culture and our religion. We were never 'Catholicized'. We still carry on our Okanagan ways."

Her fondest childhood memories are of gathering roots and berries, farming, raising chickens, trapping, hunting, and harvesting hides.

"We'd go berry picking in June, and those camps were the best. Our extended family would come to the same place and we would spend a week, ten days together. It was like a big family reunion, and as kids, we loved it!"

Jeannette's family was prominent in the community, and was often called on to host sacred ceremonies. She remembers preparing for Winter Dances, a year-long process of gathering food and gifts to give away. Those Dances were one of many ways her people gathered, prayed, and gained strength from each other.

Community, family and ceremony are all cornerstones of culture. But the heart and soul of Jeannette's culture has always been her Okanagan language. Language defines and embodies a people's unique vision of themselves; different languages reflect, and sometimes create, different realities. A fluent Okanagan speaker, Jeannette had no difficulty learning English; but she has always been acutely conscious of the different worlds defined by the two languages, and of the ways they shape both her thought and her writing.

"I learned very early that the English language is very limited. [Many words in English] don't have a true meaning; it is a dead language. For example, in English we use the word 'table.' But in Okanagan a table is really 'the thing that holds up your food.' So in Okanagan, the table does not exist without people, without a connection to something else."

> "All indigenous peoples' languages are generated by a precise geography and arise from it."

Though she writes for publication mostly in English, Jeannette goes to her own language for the true meanings of words. "My writing in English is a continuous battle against the rigidity of English," she says, " and I revel in the discoveries I make in constructing new ways to circumvent such invasive imperialism upon my tongue."[2]

For Jeannette, language is rooted in the land. She believes that "all indigenous peoples' languages are generated by a precise geography and arise from it."[3] It is the Okanagan that shapes her language and gives her voice. "I am claimed and owned by this land, this Okanagan. Voices that move within as my experience of existence do not awaken as words. Instead they move within as the colours, patterns, and movements of a beautiful, kind Okanagan landscape. They are the Grandmother voices which speak."[4]

> "I am this moment
> earth mind
> I can be nothing else

The joining of breath to sand
By water and fire
The mother body
And yet
I am small
A mote of dust
Hardly here
Unbearably without anything
To hold me
But the voices
Of grandmothers."[5]

As a child, Jeannette loved making up and telling stories. "Even at the age of 3 or 4, I had the gift of the gab. I was really encouraged by the elders. They listened to me and paid attention." She inherited her family's gift for storytelling; and she discovered at an early age that writing was just another way to tell a story. "Writing was not a big deal, it is still narrative. What's important is the story…and I saw how books were storytellers themselves."

> *"Community, family and ceremony are all cornerstones of culture. But the heart and soul of Jeannette's culture has always been her Okanagan language."*

Jeannette learned to read and write in English: first from her older sister at home, and then at school.

"It was difficult to attend school within a system in which everything was taught in English. But I had a great love for learning, and I was excited about anything, whether it was the English language or whether it was geometry."[6]

Jeannette began reading "anything I could get my hands on" and found an outlet for her creativity in both art and literature. She attended the University of Victoria and obtained a degree in Fine Arts in 1978. At the same time, Jeannette had her first opportunity to write a book that would portray and convey an Okanagan sensibility and worldview.

While developing a curriculum for children in her community, Jeannette realized that there were simply no resources available on Okanagan life before contact with Europeans. Others might simply have complained; Jeanette, like Basil Johnston, decided to write books to fill the gap. *Enwhisteetkwa/ Walk in Water*, published in 1982, "…was just intended for our Okanagan children, so they would feel part of [Canadian history]." Through the eyes of an eleven-year-old, it tells of the first encounters between Okanagan people and Europeans in 1860. *Neekna and Chamai* (1984) is the story of two young girls growing up in the Okanagan before the arrival of Europeans. Initially written to provide an Okanagan perspective on part of the history, it is now the curriculum in a number of schools in BC and went on to win the Children's Book Choice Award.

In the course of her curriculum development research, Jeanette had assembled volumes of material and information about Aboriginal people, traditional and contemporary. A non-Aboriginal consultant proposed that non-Aboriginal writers should be commissioned to develop lessons on different historical periods. That was disturbing to Jeannette, who had no intention of seeing her culture and history exploited by outsiders.

"I thought, 'how are they supposed to do this? Ridiculous. Only we can write about our history.' I said I could do it."

Looking back on that decision, Jeanette admits she didn't know what she was getting into. But she was intrigued by the challenge of trying to portray a specific period honestly, accurately, and with artistry. After two years of research and nearly two hundred interviews, Jeannette decided to tell a story – the story of a young Okanagan man on a journey of self-discovery, living through the pivotal events of the "Red Power" movement in the 1960s in Canada and the United States. **Slash,** published in 1985, is considered by many to be one of the most powerful and illuminating novels of contemporary Aboriginal life.

Thomas Kelasket is raised with the traditional values of the Okanagan people. Those values – and his life – begin to unravel under the pressure of mainstream culture and education.

> "I understood then that most Indian people have knowledge of different ways and values and that's what comes into conflict with some of the values that are taught to them in schools and by society as a whole. I realized that schools are meant to teach the young of the middle class the best way to survive their society and to maintain its system. They are not meant to instruct those who do not have the values of that society. So confusion arises inside each of the Indian kids who begin to question which value system they must live by."[7]

Severed from his roots, Thomas begins to drift across North America. His travels bring him into contact with many vivid characters, often other disenfranchised Aboriginal people. He experiences many of the seminal events of a tumultuous decade - Wounded Knee, the occupation of government offices, the American Indian Movement, the take-over of a park in northern Ontario. A growing rage builds within him, fueled by his own helplessness in the face of injustice and discrimination.

> "Sometimes I knew what it felt like to want to do something, when white kids sneered at me. Sometimes, I used to lie awake at night, wishing in the morning I would wake up and all the white people would have vanished so nobody would have to do anything about it."[8]

Each return home is a painful reminder of what he has lost by abandoning his roots - tradition, community, connectedness. Modernity has its attractions, but Thomas is being torn apart between the two worlds. His father tries to comfort and guide him:

> "I didn't go to school like you and many others. I think it's that what hurts you. You got mixed up inside. Not strong and steady like you need to be. Lots of you young people are like that. You got to find a way back, to be strong inside again. It's what you're looking for. Maybe that's what a lot of young people are looking for. That's why there is all them protests and angry demands. I guess you just got to fight for it. Nothing ever comes easy...I want you to know that we're backing you. Only use your head."[9]

Thomas eventually understands that his own culture is his only possible source of peace. Back in his community, he turns from revolution to resolution, seeking out the wisdom of medicine men, and eventually teaching his nephew and son the traditional ways.

Slash is a complex story of personal and political transformation, an evocation of an important decade in recent Aboriginal history, and a clear-sighted analysis of the effects of colonization on Aboriginal people. But the novel is far from somber; it is, in the end, an affirmation. "My purpose was not to talk about the development of pain in people," says Jeannette. "I wanted to present a picture of a healthy family, where a healthy wholeness was there, and how that could be transformed, and changed, and corrupted; where that falling apart happens, and then where that bringing back together then happens. To bring back to wholeness."[10]

Not surprisingly, *Slash* attracted a large readership and generated heated discussion among Aboriginal and non-Aboriginal readers, critics, and academics. It has been labeled a "feminist" novel, an historical novel, and a social commentary. Over the last twenty years its readership, not concerned with labels, has continued to grow. Now in its tenth printing, *Slash* is taught in Native studies, literature and high school classes across Canada.

> "For me, [poetry] forms a huge part of my life, my childhood and my everyday experience. It's a living reality."

Notwithstanding the success of her first novel, poetry has always been Jeannette's chosen medium. In 1991, she published *Breath Tracks,* her first collection.

"For me, [poetry] forms a huge part of my life, my childhood and my everyday experience. It's a living reality," says Jeannette. "It's an identification of the landscape inside me, my own internal sensibility, reactions, and understanding of all that affects me as a person. Poetry is a process in which I attempt to put into words internal things that rise up out of the subconscious, out of my spiritually and my intellect."[11]

> "...When I speak
> I attempt to bring together
> With my hands
> Gossamer thin threads of old memory
> Thoughts from the underpinnings of understanding
> Words steeped in age..."[18]

Jeannette embodies the concept of artist as activist. She sees her work – and the work of all writers – as a tool for bridging gaps between races, genders, classes and cultures.

"We need to understand one another if we're going to survive as different peoples in this world and start combating things like racism and classism and sexism. We writers have the responsibility to clarify for the world who we are, what we are, where we fit in, and what our perspective is."[13]

To that end, Jeannette has been instrumental in establishing two important institutions that reinforce and celebrate an Aboriginal sensibility and worldview.

The Enow'kin Centre had its roots in the same curriculum development project that led Jeannette to write **Slash**. As she looked for Aboriginal writers to work on development of authentic, appropriate teaching materials, she realized just how badly the educational system had failed her people. There were simply not enough Aboriginal authors with the appropriate training and experience.

When faced with a lack of children's books, Jeanette's response was to write them. When faced with a lack of authors, her response was...to teach them. So in 1981, Jeanette helped to launch the Enow'kin Centre, an Indigenous cultural, educational, ecological and creative arts post-secondary institution. "En'owkin" is an Okanagan word and concept, describing the process of coming to the best solutions possible through respectful dialogue.

> "We need to understand one another if we're going to survive as different peoples in this world and start combating things like racism and classism and sexism."

Originally an outgrowth of the curriculum project, Enow'kin "...just slowly took on a life of its own," says Jeannette. "It's very beneficial when Aboriginal people organize themselves around programs that are for our people and meet our needs." The Centre today offers a wide range of services; but it is perhaps best known for its international writing program for Aboriginal people, a course of studies that has hosted nearly all of the most influential Canadian and international Aboriginal authors - Richard Van Camp, Armand Ruffo, David Groulx, Connie Fife, and dozens of others.

But authors need publishers. And Jeannette discovered early in her writing career that most mainstream publishers were not interested in Aboriginal writers, or in a readership they perceived as a "niche" market.

"Books that sell to the public are what publishers choose to publish, because of course it's what makes a profit to keep them going," says Jeannette. " To a large extent, books for an Aboriginal audience or books on the margin are a risk economically."

Jeannette's response to the need for an Aboriginal publishing house was, of course, to help create one. In 1980 Theytus Books, named for a Salishan word which means "preserving for the sake of handing down", became Canada's first wholly Aboriginal-owned publishing house.

> **"Literary conventions constrain what we are trying to do...People should not confuse our genre with European genres and constructs."**

From the beginning, Theytus was conceived as a non-profit publisher, owned by the community and free to publish works that others could or would not. "The idea is to publish books that are important in terms of literature and for our education," says Jeannette.

Eurocentric approaches to criticism and analysis almost inevitably diminish the importance of Aboriginal literature. Theytus Books creates a space within which Aboriginal authors are free to explore cultural sensibilities and create realities beyond the literary mainstream. "Literary conventions constrain what we are trying to do," says Jeannette. "People should not confuse our genre with European genres and constructs."

Theytus Books is, by any standard, a success story. After nearly a quarter century, the company has over sixty titles in print, including important works by many of the authors profiled in this book. Despite that achievement, Jeannette believes that Aboriginal writers must continue to challenge the literary establishment. "What I learned was that there is a certain elite way of writing that is acceptable, and if you write within that framework you can be heard by the public at large. I find that to be a real dilemma in terms of what I am trying to say in my writing, because I am not willing to compromise."[14]

That challenge - the artist's quest for integrity and balance - is a key theme of Jeannette's most recent novel, **Whispering in Shadows**. Through a tapestry of literary techniques – poetry and narrative, letters and diary entries – Jeannette creates a rich, compelling and painfully real portrait of Penny Jackson, an artist and activist struggling to reconcile the demands of real life, her artistic vision, and her political and environmental activism.

In Canada, on the road, and working in indigenous communities abroad, Penny tries to cope with rising waves of despair that threaten to destroy her.

> "I feel this overwhelming anger somewhere deep inside.
> It's like all the images just begin to stack up inside. It's

like being continuously battered from inside and I can't do anything. I'm having a hard time painting because of the images. But they scream at me. I feel like I'm going to break. It's like I'm sinking. I don't know what to do."[15]

In one evocative passage, she remembers the sense of peace she associates with her grandmother, and its loss:

"When Tupa left, the shadows moved inside. It was Tupa who made the world right. She left a hole inside of me that I could find no way to fill. I let the shadows in. They whispered to me about all the things which shadows bring and I listened. I spent my time searching for light in the colours of the rainbow and tried to pull it toward me when they spoke to me. Too many shadows walk the earth and they took me away. Away from the light of each day's rising."[16]

Like Thomas in **Slash**, Penny eventually realizes that, for her, there are no political solutions. To find peace and resolution as an Aboriginal woman and as an artist, she must regain her community, and reconnect with the land to which she is linked through generations.

At one point in the novel, Penny destroys her own creations, rejecting art in favour of activism. Jeannette, too, believes that being an artist is a mixed blessing because balancing family, community and art is difficult. "For me, exploring in any art form requires the kind of liberty that sometimes society doesn't afford you and sometimes responsibility, in terms of family or work or society or your community and so on, doesn't afford you." But she feels that the artistic imagination also represents "a sacred state of being", and an essential element of our humanity.

Today Jeannette continues to speak across Canada and internationally on indigenous, literary, feminist and environmental issues. She sits on the boards and committees of many literary and indigenous organizations, and remains the Executive Director of the Enow'kin Centre. She is currently completing a new collection of poetry.

Her goal, as always, is to encourage Aboriginal people to write their stories and contribute their voices to Canadian literature.

"More Indian people have to be willing to stand up and write and not compromise. They have to take it upon themselves to lead the way and be strong about it, not give in or write the cute little fairy stories about our world view that non-Indians want in schools."[17]

In 1991, Jeannette explored her vision and concept of art in collaboration with Aboriginal architect Douglas Cardinal in a book called **The Native Creative Process.** Perhaps this statement is the clearest summary of her vision.

"At the centre of positive creative activity is the desire to bring health and enrichment into the lives of others…in Native philosophy, creative activity is a deep spiritual responsibility requiring as full an awareness as possible of its sacred nature and the necessity for pure love to be at its centre."[18]

Notes

*All excerpts from Jeannette Armstrong's books appear courtesy of **Theytus Books**, Penticton.*

[1] Jeannette Armstrong, "Threads of Old Memory," **Breath Tracks**. (Stratford: Willams-Wallace/Theytus Books, 1991) pg. 59-60.

[2] Simon Ortiz, **Speaking for the Generations: Native Writers on Writing**. Tucson: University of Arizona Press, 1998), pg. 194.

[3] Simon Ortiz, **Speaking for the Generations: Native Writers on Writing**. Tucson: University of Arizona Press, 1998), pg. 178.

[4] Ortiz, pg. 176.

[5] Jeannette Armstrong. "Grandmothers," **Gatherings III** (Penticton: Theytus Books, 1992)

[6] **Telling It:** Women and Language Across Cultures, Vancouver: Press Gang 1990, pg. 25.

[7] Jeannette Armstrong, **Slash** (Penticton: Theytus Books, 1985) pg. 212.

[8] **Slash**, pg. 31.

[9] **Slash**, pg. 87.

[10] "Jeannette Armstrong," Hartmut Lutz. **Contemporary Challenges: Conversations with Canadian Native Writers**, Saskatoon: Fifth House, 1991) pg. 19.

[11] Williamson, Janice. "Jeannette Armstrong," **Sounding Differences: Conversations with 17 Canadian Women Writers**. (Toronto: University of Toronto, 1993) pg. 20.

[12] Jeannette Armstrong, "Threads of Old Memory," **Breath Tracks**, pg. 59.

[13] Williamson, Janice, **Sounding Differences**, pg. 22.

[14] Jeannette Armstrong, "Writing from a Native Woman's Perspective," *In the Feminine: Women and Words Conference Proceedings*, 1983. (Alberta: Longspoon Press, 1985) pg. 55.

[15] Jeannette Armstrong, *Whispering in Shadows.* (Penticton: Theytus Books, 2000) pg. 187.

[16] Jeannette Armstrong, *Whispering in Shadows*, pg. 285.

[17] Jeannette Armstrong, *In the Feminine*, pg. 57.

[18] Jeannette Armstrong, Douglas Cardinal *The Native Creative Process.* (Penticton: Theytus Books, 1991) pg. 106.

Major Works by Jeannette Armstrong

Breath Tracks. Stratford: Williams-Wallace/Theytus Books, 1991.

Enwhisteetkwa, Walk in Water. Penticton: Friesen Printers, 1982.

The Native Creative Process. Penticton: Theytus Books, 1991.

Neekna and Chemai. Penticton: Theytus Books, 1984.

Slash. Penticton: Theytus Books, 1985.

Whispering in Shadows. Penticton: Theytus Books, 2000.

Numerous other poems, essays, oratory, and audio-visual products in books and anthologies across North America.

Armand Garnet Ruffo

Armand Garnet Ruffo is a unique artist – an accomplished writer who combines the passion and sensibilities of a poet with the disciplined curiosity of an historian. This unusual approach has enabled him to bring new insight to famous characters, real and legendary, and illuminate their lives with new meaning.

Armand was born in the small community of Chapleau in northern Ontario. There were few books in his family's home while he was growing up. However, there *was* a poet in the household.

"My grandmother, although she had little formal education, wrote poetry. At the time, I wasn't really interested in poetry - or writing for that matter - but as I got older, I seemed to gravitate towards it. Poetry seemed to come naturally to me. And history also began to interest me - namely, who gets to tell it. I guess I also get this from my grandmother, who was an historian for our family, and a real wealth of knowledge."

Armand spent his early years hunting, trapping and fishing. His life, however, was far from solitary; working in the bush for a Cree outfitter brought him into contact with a wide range of people from "outside". And while he much preferred the outdoors to attending school, he was always an avid reader.

"I became interested in books at quite an early age. I remember my mother buying me books for Christmas, and bringing me to the public library. Even though she didn't have much education herself, she understood the value of knowledge."

Although he had always thought of himself as too much of a dreamer to be a good student, Armand graduated from high school and was accepted at York University in Toronto. His initial plan was to study biology. When an elective course in photography failed to fit into his schedule, he decided to register for a creative writing course instead. It was his first opportunity to explore his identity as an Aboriginal person through writing, a challenge he found far from easy.

"At first I was trying to imitate all these famous dead writers... the professor gave us an anthology... I tried to copy their styles. I remember reading Yeats, but I'd never even been to Ireland! I'd write a line or two and stop. I couldn't write. I was blocked."

Then his professor advised Armand to write about himself and the things that really mattered to him.

"Suddenly I started writing this poetry about my Native roots, and where I came from, and what it was like to find yourself lost in the city. My professor said, 'this is it, this is your material.'"

Armand continued to write poetry throughout university, but strictly for his own eyes. In 1977, he began working for an Aboriginal magazine called "The Native Perspective". Through its literary pages, he began to read many of the emerging young native voices – amateur writers from all walks of life, experimenting with form and content, more interested in making a statement than in becoming professional writers.

"I was interested in the poetry that was being sent in, especially from Native prisoners. I thought it was important. What struck me was that 90% of the work was from just regular folk. They were your relatives and neighbours, grandmothers writing at a kitchen table - including my own grandmother! I published her poetry that summer. It was the first time she'd ever been published. I can still see the look of astonishment and pride on her face. That was very inspirational for me."

> "I was interested in the poetry that we being sent in, especially from Native prisoners. I thought it was important. What struck me was that 90% of the work was from just regular folk. They were your relatives and neighbours, grandmothers writing at a kitchen table."

Still writing and still unpublished, Armand found employment as an editor for the Native Council of Canada. "It was then that I began submitting my own work to various Native newspapers and magazines. At the time, there was an advocacy for publishing Native material, and they were very accepting."

Aboriginal writing was attracting growing interest in publishing circles in the late 1970s, and that gave Armand enough confidence to submit his poetry to literary magazines across Canada. But much to his dismay, his submissions were rejected. Discouraged and disillusioned, he almost quit writing. And then he met the award-winning playwright George Ryga, at that time writer-in-residence at the University of Ottawa.

"I bundled up my poems and sent them to him. Not only did he read them, but he called me up and said he wanted to go through my work with me. So we met and talked about writing. That's when he gave me some advice that I've never forgotten. He said, 'whatever you do, don't stop writing, no matter what anybody says'. So I continued."

Armand acknowledges the significance of that meeting, and of Ryga's advice, in a tribute published as part of his first collection.

> I also think of you visiting me and
> Going through my words. Not
> One for compliment, idle talk, you
> Came to offer advice. You said poetry is a gift...
>
> You said our responsibility
> Is to speak. To speak for those who cannot.
> A child grows with circles in his eyes
> And looks for direction. Some find it.
> Some do not.[1]

Encouraged, Armand continued to write, and gradually his poems began to appear in magazines and journals. Initially his work found greater acceptance in the United States than in Canada. But Native literature continued to attract growing critical interest and readership through the 1980s; both mainstream and Aboriginal publishers and periodicals were seeking out new authors. In 1989, Heather Hodgson, a guest editor for Theytus Books, an Aboriginal publishing house based in Penticton, B.C., read Armand's poetry in an American journal and invited him to contribute to **Seventh Generation: Contemporary Native Writing**, the first Aboriginal anthology in Canada.

"Suddenly, I had two months to write, and was among other aspirinig writers. It was the first time in my life that I actually began to think of myself as writer."

That same year, Armand accepted a scholarship to the Banff Centre for the Arts. For the first time, he was to have an opportunity to focus exclusively on his own writing.

"It was an important move for me," Armand says. "Suddenly, I had two months to write, and was among other aspiring writers. It was the first time in my life that I actually began to think of myself as a writer, because I was being treated as one by writers like Adele Wiseman."

From Banff, Armand moved to the University of Windsor, where he studied under Alistair MacLeod, one of Canada's most honoured authors. It was an inspiring and prolific time for Armand; he continued to write poetry, scripted a play, and prepared the first draft of a book about Archie Belaney – better known as Grey Owl.

Following his graduation in 1993, Armand move to Penticton, B.C., where he taught at the Enow'kin Centre, a First Nations fine arts institution. One year later, he completed and published **Opening in the Sky,** his first book of poetry.

> Poetry
> Makes me want to write poetry
> Exotic disease I guess,
> Butterfly palpitations
> Bursting across the kitchen table
> Fragrance of sweetgrass
> And wild mint wafting into the room...
>
> Nothing to do with
> I can do better
> Nothing like that, this honest desire
> That kicks
> Like a new born calf
> Jumping up and disappearing
> Into its own geography.[2]

Opening in the Sky draws images from Armand's Ojibway heritage and themes from his life. There are poems of the land, of struggle, of love and of loss. And there are poems of history, exploring the minds and lives of characters as diverse as Almighty Voice and Christopher Columbus. This excerpt speaks of Duncan Campbell Scott, a poet and Indian Affairs bureaucrat from the turn of the century:

> Some whisper this man lives in a house of many rooms,
> Has a cook and a maid and even a gardener
> To cut his grass and water his flowers.
> Some don't care, they don't like the look of him.
> They say he asks many questions but
> Doesn't wait to listen. Asks
> Much about yesterday, little about today
> And acts as if he knows tomorrow.
> Others don't like the way he's always busy writing
> Stuff in the notebook he carries. Him,
> He calls it poetry
> And says it will make us who are doomed
> Live forever.[3]

History is too often written in a single voice. Much of Armand's writing attempts to recreate history as dialogue between multiple perspectives, and to reintroduce the voices of Aboriginal writers to that dialogue.

"There is power in naming. Words have power. Words were always considered sacred in Native culture and they give power. What we have to do is claim our history as Aboriginal history…As a child I had some bad experiences with Canadian history in terms of Aboriginal people. I look at Canadian history and I say, well, how do I see it? How can I rewrite it or give another perspective?"

Following the publication of his first volume of poetry, Armand returned in the early 1990s to a project he had been mulling over for many years – the story of Grey Owl.

Born in 1888, Archie Belaney was a middle class Englishman raised on romantic stories about Indians and the Canadian wilderness. He moved to Canada in 1906, and soon found work as a guide and trapper. As his hair grew longer and his skin darkened, he began to claim Aboriginal ancestry; and he was, in fact, adopted by several Aboriginal families, and was given the name "Wa-Sha-Quon-Asin ", or Grey Owl. Over the years, he became an ardent conservationist, author, lecturer and advocate. Grey Owl's true identity was exposed after his death in 1938.

> *"[Grey Owl]certainly made an important contribution to the idea of what it was to be Aboriginal in Canada…it was a story that had to be told, because his life is about that search, that need to be secure and find one's own identity."*

Many of Grey Owl's early years in Canada were spent in northern Ontario, in and around the town of Biscotasing, where he was welcomed into the Espaniel family and learned the traditional life of the Ojibway.

"He showed up in Bisco as part Apache," says Armand, remembering his family's stories of Belaney. "At that time my great grandfather was a community leader…and Archie went to live with him because he had prominence in the Native community. He was adopted by my family."

> One day we see him sprawled outside his shack
> Shivering, too weak even to get up and feed himself,
> And my wife says, Look at the pitiful thing won't you?
> He's got to get back into the bush, I say,
> And my son puts him over his shoulder
> And we take him to our camp
> On Indian Lake.[4]

The family had many stories about Grey Owl – especially Armand's grandmother, who collected photographs, newspaper clippings, and personal anecdotes. It was a natural subject for Armand, combining history, poetry, and an absorbing exploration of culture and identity.

"Here was somebody trying to be someone other than who he was. He certainly made an important contribution to the idea of what it was to be Aboriginal in Canada. It's a complex issue, appropriation and assimilation. It was a story that had to be told, because his life is about that search, that need to be secure and find one's own identity."

In the north
A man's past
Is his own

Archie
Relishes
The thought

It allows
Possibilities
Never expected

> In the north
> A man's past
> Is his imagination
>
> Archie relishes
> The possibility
> To be

> > In the north
> > Archie relishes
> > The welcome.[5]

Grey Owl/Archie Belaney was never sure of his own identity. Armand believes it was that uncertainty that eventually killed him.

> In August alone, a thousand visitors
> Make the trip to Beaver Lodge,
> Young and old alike, Americans,
> Europeans, even a Viscount and a Major,
> All while I'm busy preparing my lectures
> For my second British tour.

> They say a criminal always returns
> To the scene of the crime. Certainly
> This has nothing to do with me.
> Still, what I want to know is
> Does he get away with it?[6]

Though Grey Owl struggled all his life to define his own identity, Armand believes that many Aboriginal people now accept Grey Owl as an early advocate.

"You have to remember that at that time, it was illegal to leave some reserves without a pass. Aboriginal people couldn't hire a lawyer. That too was illegal. We were basically captives of the government. Then along comes this articulate man who is proud to be Native, who speaks on behalf of the people any chance he gets, and can possibly help change things. I think people forget how much he was influenced by the Native community."

The themes of history and identity were further explored in Armand's next collection of poetry, **At Geronimo's Grave**. Geronimo, an extraordinary spiritual and intellectual leader, fought for most of his life to defend the Apache way of life in the face of encroaching American settlers in the southwest United States. Feared and pursued by white and Spanish settlers throughout his life, he became a potent symbol of courage and cultural survival to Aboriginal people. His many escapes and his eloquence and passion in speaking about the brutal treatment of his people are legendary.

While attending a writer's conference in Oklahoma in 1989, Armand visited Geronimo's grave, and was deeply moved by the experience.

"I just couldn't get it out of my head. So I just thought of writing a poem about Geronimo. After that I said, I need to write another one…and as I wrote about Geronimo I realized that I was writing more about myself… and our struggle to accept our place in Canada as Aboriginal people."

Geronimo finally surrendered in 1886. He was sent to prison at Fort Sill, in Oklahoma, where he died in of pneumonia on February 17, 1909, as a prisoner of war far from his homeland. For Armand, Geronimo's struggle epitomizes six centuries of struggle by Aboriginal people, from first contact to the present day.

"People often say 'Why are you writing about Aboriginal people when you could easily blend in? Why are you crying? Accept your losses, it was a long time ago – we're all equal.' Implying that I should forget my history and just be like them. When I started reading Geronimo's autobiography, I saw how he'd struggled and endured. What he went through is unimaginable today, but he never gave up. In fact, he's been called the last of the holdouts. I saw his life was also a metaphor for the struggle that is still going on. Aboriginal people don't want to blend in and forget who they are, where they come from, and become like the so-called 'immigrant society'. We have a whole pre-contact history with rights arising from that history. That's what Geronimo was fighting for."

> To you who braved
> The good fight
> Your last horse shot
> From under you
> In the Arizona desert
>
> You who did all you could
> To create destruction
> When all you saw
> Was destruction
> Of the old way of life

I ask here at the end
Of the twentieth century
As I contemplate surrender
To you who lived
Its beginning

What did you see
    When you finally signed?
What did you hear
    When they spoke of progress?
What did you feel
    When they made their promises?
What did you mean
    When you said you understood?[7]

At Geronimo's Grave contains some of Armand's most political work to date.
It explores the contrast between the complex, unknowable, genuine hero,
and the pop icon Geronimo has come to represent, an ever-shifting series of
stereotypes about what Aboriginal people "really are" - bloodthirsty villains,
noble savages, brave warriors, tragic victims.

"When I considered the dominant culture's portrayal of Aboriginal people, I
realized that Geronimo, the myth-maker, embodied these stereotypical
perceptions. We start with being considered useful by the first settlers, the
Hudson Bay, though still savages; then, the negative trouble-maker stereotypes
come into vogue of a people blocking progress; then, we get the down-and-
out skid row label of a people who can't handle civilization, then, when (the
movie) *Dances with Wolves* came out Native people were popular again. This
evolving perception is similar as to how society looked at Geronimo. The
more I thought about it, the more I realized that there is intersection between
Geronimo's life, Native people in general, and my life, to some extent."

Dance to hold on
To who you are.

It's what you do
With half your life in prison.

You dance
The distant land
Of your Apache home.

And become a show
A curious spectacle
For the city folks
Who come to see
Authentic savage custom.

What they do not see is your spirit
Dance to hold on...[8]

In 2001, Armand drew inspiration from the darker side of Ojibway mythology to fashion a modern tale of power and healing. With the assistance of the National Arts Centre's "On The Verge" workshop and Native Earth Performing Arts Inc., he completed and staged his first play, **A Windigo Tale**.

Doris is a middle-aged Aboriginal woman caught between two worlds. Born into a traditional Native household but raised in a Christian residential school, she grows up denying her roots, suffering indignity and abuse in an imposed culture. The intergenerational legacy of residential school manifests itself when her husband sexually abuses their only daughter, Lily, and Doris is powerless.

Years later, angry and embittered by the past wrongs, Lily arrives for a visit with her boyfriend David at the invitation of Doris' auntie Evelyn. When Lily chances upon her father's clothes, she unwittingly unleashes the mythical, cannibalistic Windigo. A lifetime of suppressed pain explodes between the two women.

"I wanted to use the old to express something new. Stories change, they evolve...I wanted to bring relevance into the Windigo story so that it's not a dead story from the past, but something that's relevant today."

Shattered by the knowledge of her failure to protect Lily from a childhood of chronic abuse, and frantic to protect her daughter and right past wrongs, Doris struggles with a crisis of faith. As Christianity fails her, she instinctively turns to her Native culture. At the play's climax, Doris convinces David to don her husband's clothing, evoking and incarnating the Windigo spirit so that she can strip it of its power.

In Ojibway culture, the Windigo is a cannibal, a creature that invades and possesses an individual, driving them insane with the lust for human flesh. The tell-tale sign of Windigo possession is the transformation of a person's heart to ice, the destruction of human emotion. In Armand's play, sexual abuse becomes a form of cannibalism, dehumanizing and degrading its victim and consuming their capacity to feel, to be fully human.

Lily comes up behind Doris and stands by the stove. Doris turns around and is startled by her.

DORIS
Oh, my goodness, you gave me a fright.

LILY
(She puts her hands over the stove.) Most times I feel

frozen inside.

DORIS
Thought I'd make you a good breakfast.

LILY
I can't get warm.

DORIS
(Staring at her for a moment.) Supposed to be a cold one today... but nothing like heat from a woodstove.

LILY
Like I could step in front of a car and it would shatter me.

DORIS
(Ignoring her. Quickly interrupting, rubbing her arms)
Cold's bad for my arthritis.

LILY
But you already know don't you mother?

DORIS
So much to know these days.[9]

Armand's startling reinvention of the ancient Windigo story with a contemporary setting and characters is disturbingly effective. It evokes the power of a traditional archetype, and affirms some dark and timeless truths about humanity.

"I wanted to use the old to express something new. Stories change, they evolve. We're not static, cultures are not static. We take old elements and make them new. I wanted to bring relevance into the Windigo story so that it's not a dead story from the past, but something that's relevant today."

Armand Ruffo's work is a rich and compelling synthesis of poetic vision, historical fact and mythic scale. He is currently writing the screenplay for a film version of **A Windigo Tale** and completing a new collection of poetry. He also teaches Aboriginal literature at Carleton University in Ottawa, where he shares his enthusiasm for the new wave of native authors with his students.

"I think we're in a very exciting time right now. There's a whole cultural renewal going on, and literature is part of that. It's nice to know our literature is becoming an integral part of the Canadian landscape and is being accepted. There are a lot of new developments and new voices, and I'm sure there will be a lot more to come."

Notes

Excerpts from Armand Ruffo's books appear with permission of the following publishers:

Opening in the Sky, Theytus Books, Penticton.
Grey Owl, At Geronimo's Grave, Coteau Books, Regina.

[1] Armand Ruffo, "Some (for George Ryga)", **Opening in the Sky**, (Penticton: Theytus Books, 1994), p. 46.

[2] Armand Ruffo. "Poetry", **Opening in the Sky.** (Penticton: Theytus Books, 1994), p. 68.

[3] Armand Ruffo. "For Duncan Campbell Scott," **Opening in the Sky.** (Penticton: Theytus Books, 1994), p. 25.

[4] Armand Ruffo, "Alex Espaniel, 1920," **Grey Owl: The Mystery of Archie Belaney**. (Regina: Coteau Books, 1996), p. 33.

[5] Armand Ruffo, "North 1906," **Grey Owl: The Mystery of Archie Belaney.** (Regina: Coteau Books, 1996), p. 12.

[6] Armand Ruffo, "Grey Owl, 1937," **Grey Owl: The Mystery of Archie Belaney.** (Regina: Coteau Books, 1996), p. 155.

[7] Armand Ruffo, "Contemplating Surrender," **At Geronimo's Grave.** (Regina: Coteau Books, 2001), p. 15.

[8] Armand Ruffo, "Dance to Hold On," **At Geronimo's Grave.** (Regina: Coteau Books, 2001), p. 89.

[9] Armand Ruffo, **A Windigo Tale**. Draft manuscript. 2003. p. 10.

Major Works by Armand Ruffo

At Geronimo's Grave. Regina: Coteau Books, 2001.
Grey Owl: The Mystery of Archie Belany. Regina: Coteau Books, 1996.
Opening in the Sky. Pentiction: Theytus Books, 1994.

Maria Campbell

"Don't let anyone tell you that anything is impossible,
because if you believe honestly in your heart that there's
something better for you, then it will all come true. Go out
there and find what you want and take it, but always
remember who you are and why you want it."[1]

Mother and grandmother. Storyteller. Activist. Novelist. Community worker. Maria Campbell has worn a lot of labels. But her great-grandmother's wise words, the words of her beloved "Cheechum", have always been her anchor. It's been a long road: but today Maria is acknowledged as one of Canada's most respected Métis artists, and honoured for her tireless commitment to both her writing, and to raising awareness of Métis life and culture.

Born in northern Saskatchewan "during a spring blizzard in April 1940"[2], Maria grew up in what she describes as a happy, secure and traditional family, a home filled with laughter and stories. The oldest of five children, Maria learned from her father to hunt and trap, while her mother instilled in her a love of literature and stories.

"She loved books and music and spent many hours reading to us from a collection of books her father gave us. I grew up on Shakespeare, Dickens, Sir Walter Scott and Longfellow. My imagination was stirred by the stories in Mom's books."[3]

She was equally inspired by the raucous evenings of conversation, gossip and laughter told around the kitchen table. Long nights of family folklore, ghost stories, anecdotes about friends and community members – all part of the way that Métis spend time together and affirm their culture, as families and as a people. Maria carries memories of those evenings with her to this day.

> **Characters, situations and voices from those childhood evenings around the kitchen table would populate Maria's work for years.**

"Métis people are storytellers. I think all Aboriginal people are storytellers. I grew up in a small isolated community and I didn't have a radio until I was 8 or 9; so storytellers were a really important part of my growing up. Everything that I learned as a child - lessons, values, traditions - all came through stories."

Characters, situations and voices from those childhood evenings around the kitchen table would populate Maria's work for years; and decades later, many of those stories would form the heart of her most recent short story collection. But between that happy childhood and Maria's life today lay the difficult years described in Maria's groundbreaking autobiography, **Halfbreed**.

It began as a letter. A friend suggested that if Maria needed to talk to someone, she should write try writing to herself. Two thousand pages later, Maria put the letter aside. It was only at the urging of another friend that she began to see her writing as something others might share. **Halfbreed**'s almost painful intimacy and honesty may be due to the fact that it was originally written for an audience of one.

Published in 1973, **Halfbreed** chronicles Maria's life with her family until her early 30s. Touching and unflinching, it is a heartbreaking look at the collapse of a young woman's life. After her mother dies, twelve year old Maria tries to keep her family together. In her desperation, she marries a white man at the age of fifteen, hoping this will allow her to keep her siblings with her. But her abusive husband contacts Social Services; her brothers and sisters are taken away to foster homes, and the family is dispersed. Abandoned by her husband, Maria ends up a drug addict on the streets of Vancouver.

At one point Maria admits to hating her own family and people. But her Cheechum reminds her of responsibility, and her power to bring about change for the Métis community. After deriding her family for their poverty, her great-grandmother describes what happened as the Halfbreed people moved west in search of freedom.

> "They fought each other just as you are fighting your
> mother and father today. The white man saw that that was
> a more powerful weapon than anything else with which to
> beat the Halfbreeds, and he used it and still does today.
> Already they are using it on you. They try to make you
> hate your people." She stood up then and said, "I will beat
> you each time I hear you talk as you did. If you don't like

what you have, then stop fighting your parents and do something about it yourself."

Those powerful words helped Maria to define and pursue her path in life as an artist, an activist and a community worker.

Shot through with moments of insight, wit, courage, and beauty, **Halfbreed** is, ultimately, a story of redemption through courage, culture, and faith in self.

The publication of **Halfbreed** had a tremendous impact in Canada. Its artistic and commercial success inspired a new wave of Aboriginal writers like Lee Maracle (**Bobbi Lee**) and Beatrice Culleton (**April Raintree**), who credit Maria Campbell for influencing their work. But Maria's goal had never been to launch a literary movement. Her only intention in writing the book was to "stay alive." "I see it as being an act of survival. I had to live. I didn't want to die."

> She feels privileged to have been part of a movement in Aboriginal writing, linking her work, and that of other authors, with the literature of oppression worldwide.

She feels privileged to have been part of a movement in Aboriginal writing, linking her work, and that of other authors, with the literature of oppression worldwide. "I look at the literature of other colonized people, and the early writing is always painful. But it shows people's survival. And out of that pain comes amazing things."

Halfbreed had a powerful impact on mainstream audiences, for the first time introducing many readers to the life of Canada's "forgotten people", the Métis. And that was Maria's intention, set out in the preface of **Halfbreed:** "I write this to tell you what it is like to be a Halfbreed woman in our country. I want to tell you about the joys and sorrows, the oppressing poverty, the frustrations and the dreams."[4]

The early 1970s were a time of explosive political development in Aboriginal communities across North America, and Maria's book immediately found an audience interested in exploring the reality behind the headlines.

"I think the book did well because it was published in 1973, because we had come through Wounded Knee and because there was an awakening in Canada of Aboriginal people, of Halfbreed people. It forced people to come inside my kitchen instead of looking at me from outside my window. I think that because it was medicine for me, it must have touched people."

Halfbreed was shaped by the events of Maria's own life: the inspiration for her next work was also close to home. When her daughter came home from school one day and announced that she hated Indians, Maria, not surprisingly, was upset.

"I went charging over to the school ...I went to confront this one teacher. She showed me the text she had been using, and my daughter couldn't identify with that. The other kids made fun of her when she said she was Native, so she hated being Native. I had a talk with the teacher, and she said there's nothing else in the library. And there wasn't!"

Appalled by the lack of appropriate, accurate information about Aboriginal people available in the schools, Maria took the most direct action conceivable: she wrote **People of the Buffalo** and **Riel's People**.

People of the Buffalo is about the lives and culture of the Plains Cree people. It illustrates and affirms a way of life that was innovative, practical, and deeply fulfilling. It is also a passionate argument for the retention of traditional values.

> "Today, Indian people are fighting back using the laws that almost destroyed them, but most important of all, they are going back to their spiritual way of life. That is the most important weapon of all: to know who you are and where you come from."[5]

A question from her 4-year-old grandson ("Where did Fire come from?") led Maria to write **Little Badger and the Fire Spirit**, another children's book, in 1977. Maria has "a big pile of children's stories" that one day may be published; but given the number of talented Aboriginal authors now writing for children, she decided to explore other creative areas – including film.

In 1978, Maria wrote the script for **The Red Dress**, an NFB film about a young non-status girl struggling to balance the traditional life of her family with the allure of the modern, "white" world. The experience was valuable, but not artistically satisfying: Maria found she had much less control over the production than an author has over a book. The film evolved in directions she was not happy with, but Maria had learned her lesson. Her subsequent film, a documentary called **The Road Allowance People**, dramatized Métis culture and life, highlighting the importance of storytelling and music in the tradition. And this time, she retained creative control.

Her film work emphasizes the fact that Maria's goals go beyond just writing. Through her work, she wants to raise awareness of Métis issues, and win recognition for the contribution made by Métis people to this country. Writing is only one means to that end.

I don't think of myself as a writer. My work is in the community. Writing is just one of the tools that I use in my work as an organizer.

"I don't think of myself as a writer. My work is in the community. Writing is just one of the tools that I use in my work as an organizer. If I think that something else would work better, then I do it. I do video, I do film, and I do oral storytelling."[6]

In the early 1980s, after seeing a performance of the Aboriginal play **Almighty Voice**, Maria was inspired to try her hand at theatre. Working with Paul

Thompson, director of Theatre Passe Muraille, and with stage actor Linda Griffiths, Maria began to develop *Jessica,* a play with elements loosely based on her life. The play, when it was finally staged in 1986, was a critical success and won several awards; but the real drama took place behind the scenes. More than any other medium, theatrical production challenges artists, often with widely disparate styles and visions, to collaborate in a complex creative process fraught with challenges – and *Jessica* was no exception. Rather than simply publish their script, Maria and Linda Griffiths decided to tell the story of the making of the play in the form of a dramatic dialogue. ***The Book of Jessica: a theatrical transformation*** is a shocking and challenging work that explores race, art, anger, and identity. Linda and Maria's voices alternate as they talk about the contradictions inherent in a white actress playing a mixed-blood woman who is exposing her own life story and watching it performed by someone else.

> MARIA: "Do you know how appalled I was at myself when I heard you say those things? You were playing back my own self-hatred. I was making a joke about something that really hurt me, and when Jessica said those things she was so flip, and I'd think, 'How could I say something like that?' And I'd think about how much I hated myself, and I'd get angry, and then would come the questions, the political analysis: 'How did that happen?' It was those white people that came along and did this to us, made us hate ourselves. Then I'd look up and there you'd be, one of them."[7]

In another conversation, Maria and Linda argue about the power of art and how true art steals something from people but then returns it to them, transformed into something beautiful. Linda finally agrees; then Maria decries the theft of Aboriginal people and traditions by artists who do not give anything back.

> LINDA: I'm a thief. And it's not just Native people I've stolen from...I'm a professional thief.
>
> MARIA: That's what art is, Linda.
>
> LINDA: I've felt that you hated art.
>
> MARIA: Art has become a bad thing. I keep telling you that. Today, most art is ugly because it's not responsible to the people it steals from. Real, honest-to-God true art steals from the people. It's a thief. It comes in...it walks off with all your stuff, but then it gives it back to you and heals you, empowers you, and it's beautiful. 75% of the art that's out there steals, but it doesn't give anything back...it takes your stuff and it hangs it up on the wall and it says, "Look what I've done. Isn't that wonderful, I'm an

artist." It's all pure ego, and when you say that maybe I'm the healer and you're the artist, that's bullshit. If you're an artist and you're not a healer, then you're not an artist—not in my sense of what art is. Art is the most powerful…it's the main healing tool. The artist in the old communities was the most sacred person of all.[8]

At the end of the process, both Maria and Linda agreed that they were still not happy or comfortable with each other. But they had learned. As Maria said: "Angry or not, I feel good, and that's a lot better than feeling angry and bad."[9]

The **Jessica** experience had been exhausting, and for a time Maria put her energy into community and political projects, always with the goal of working as "an artist who heals." An important part of Maria's commitment has always been working with women, in prison and on the streets. Through workshops, she encourages them to reclaim and be proud of their heritage, as part of their healing.

When Maria did begin to think about publishing another book, her goal was clear. She had been remembering those long evenings of storytelling. "When Métis people get together", she says, "the kitchen is always full of stories." Her next book would capture the spirit of those evenings, and record some of their best tales. She had attempted several times to translate and write down some of the stories she remembered from her youth; but they just didn't work on paper, and she had reluctantly decided that those wonderful tales were simply meant to remain part of a purely oral tradition. Then one day her father came to visit, and began telling stories while cooking moose meat for his grandchildren.

"My kids were sitting around and…he was telling them stories in his English …I was standing in the doorway into the kitchen and I was observing, I was sort of the film maker, the writer. I was observing. I heard him for the first time in a different way. I didn't hear his story; I heard for the first time his use of the language. I don't know how to explain what happened to me, because that was a really important moment in my work for my stories."

> "I heard [my father] for the first time in a different way. I didn't hear his story; I heard for the first time his use of the language. I don't know how to explain what happened to me, because that was a really important moment in my work for my stories."

Inspired, Maria began immediately to write down a story, and realized what had been missing. "When I wrote it in the language that we spoke at home, that's what was missing, the way that we use English. The stories came alive and I captured something in them…(the stories) fell on the page like poetry."

"Well you kno
dis Ole Arcand
he was one hell of a fiddle player.
Boy he can play anyting

An He makes up hees own songs too.
He always have a good story about how he got dah
Song.

He says he got one song from dah wind at Batoche
Anudder one
He say dat his horse he give it to him.
But one good song he have
Dat was da bes one of all.
He call dat One La Beau Sha Shoo."[10]

"What I had to do was throw aside all of the things that I had been taught about writing - that you put commas here, and you do all of these things - and I just forgot about them. I listened instead for the way that the storytellers told the story. They didn't stop and take a breath or a comma where it was suppose to go properly. They just spoke it. So that's what I did."

The result was **Stories of the Road Allowance People**, a joyful, eclectic collection of Métis tales, full of raunchy imagery and superstitious legends. The stories and characters come alive through use of what Maria calls "village English", the authentic voices of Métis storytellers. "It's the rhythm," says Maria. "If I change the rhythm, then the spirit moves out of the story." But the spirit never leaves these stories. Maria has come full circle, and captured the magic of those late-night kitchen sessions.

Today, Maria continues to share her stories through the storytelling workshops for Aboriginal youth and through her work with the University of Saskatchewan and the Gabriel Dumont Institute. She spends her summers in the bush, in what she calls "an old road allowance shack in the woods", where she chops wood and hauls water – a place for reflection, creativity, and healing.

> *The stories and characters come alive through use of what Maria calls "village English", the authentic voices of Métis storytellers.*

Living a life split between the bush and the city, the traditional and modern, Maria has come to terms with change. Métis people have always been adaptors, and she is confident that today's Aboriginal youth will find their way in the modern world while retaining the traditions and culture that define them and give them strength.

"I think that the important thing that we talk about when we say 'reclaiming our tradition' is - what do we mean? Spirit is something that we can all have. If we've lost that in ourselves, we can find that. But don't ever let anyone make you believe that the tree and the grass in the city are less sacred than what is out on the land…we have to honour the place where our kids are at…Everything is going to be okay. I think it's going to be different - but it was different a hundred years ago. Times change. We need to use the tools to make the culture richer."

For Maria, writing is a tool, one of the many ways in which she works to make her culture richer, to share a Métis awareness of the world with those around her, and to change people's perceptions.

"I write because I want to change things. I want a better life for my grandkids. I want them to be able to feel good about who they are, and go to school and see that the things that their grandparents had are valued."

NOTES

Excerpts from Maria Campbell's books have been quoted with permission of the following publishers:

Halfbreed— McClelland & Stewart Ltd., Toronto: *The Canadian Publishers.*
Stories of the Road Allowance People—Theytus Books, Penticton.

[1] Maria Campbell, **Halfbreed.** (Toronto: McClelland and Stewart, 1973) 98.

[2] **Halfbreed**, 16.

[3] **Halfbreed**, 14.

[4] **Halfbreed**, 2.

[5] Maria Campbell, **People of the Buffalo.** (Vancouver: JJ Douglas, 1976) 47.

[6] Hartmut Lutz, **Contemporary Challenges. Conversations with Canadian Native Authors.** (Saskatoon: Fifth House Publishers, 1991) 41.

[7] Linda Griffiths and Maria Campbell, **The Book of Jessica: A Theatrical Transformation**. (Toronto: Coach House Press, 1989) 31.

[8] **Book of Jessica**, 83-84.

[9] **Book of Jessica**, 112.

[10] Maria Campbell, *Stories of the Road Allowance People.* (Penticton: Theytus Books, 1995) 55-56.

Major Works by Maria Campbell

The Book of Jessica: a theatrical transformation. With Linda Griffiths. Toronto: Coach House Press, 1989.

Halfbreed. Toronto: McClelland & Stewart, 1973.

Little Badger and the Fire Spirit. Toronto: McClelland & Stewart, 1977.

People of the Buffalo: How the Métis Lived. Vancouver: J.J. Douglas, 1976.

Riel's People : How the Métis lived. Vancouver: Douglas & McIntyre, 1978.

Stories of the Road Allowance People. Penticton: Theytus Books, 1995.